Information Systems Engineeri

SSADM and Client/Server Applications

LONDON: HMSO

Acknowledgements

The assistance of Parity Plc in the preparation of this volume under contract to CCTA is gratefully acknowledged. The assistance of BIS Training in this volume's review process is also gratefully acknowledged.

© **Crown copyright 1994**

Applications for reproduction should be made to HMSO

First published 1995

ISBN: 0 11 330624 5

For further information regarding CCTA products please contact:

CCTA Library
Rosebery Court
St Andrews Business Park
Norwich
NR7 0HS
01603 704930

Foreword

The **Information Systems Engineering Library** provides guidance on managing and carrying out Information Systems Engineering activities. In the IS lifecycle, Information Systems Engineering takes place once the IS strategy has been defined. It is concerned with the development and ongoing improvement of information systems up to the operational stage, and their maintenance whilst in operational use.

The Information Systems Engineering Library complements other CCTA products, in particular the project management method, PRINCE, and the systems analysis and design method, SSADM.

Volumes in the Information Systems Engineering Library are of interest to varying levels of staff from IS directors to IS providers, helping them to improve the quality and productivity of their IS development work. Some volumes in this library should also be of interest to business managers, IS users and those involved in market testing, whose business operations depend on having effective IS support by means of Information Systems Engineering activities.

The Information Systems Engineering Library also complements other related CCTA publications, in particular the Programme and Project Management Library, the Information Management Library for data management issues, the IT Infrastructure Library for operational issues and the IS Planning Subject Guides for strategic issues.

CCTA welcomes customer views on the Information Systems Engineering Library publications. Please send your comments to:

Information Systems Engineering Group
CCTA
Rosebery Court
St Andrews Business Park
Norwich
NR7 0HS

SSADM and Client/Server Applications

Contents

		Page
	Foreword	3

Chapter

1	Introduction	9

    1.1   Purpose of this volume
    1.2   Scope
    1.3   Who should read this volume
    1.4   Structure
    1.5   Reader's guide

2	Concepts	13

    2.1   What is client/server?
    2.2   The client/server relationship can be hierarchic
    2.3   Examples of clients and servers
    2.4   A cross-section of an application
    2.5   Key issues for designers of client/server systems
    2.6   Examples of client/server partitioning
    2.7   Design differences for transaction processing
    2.8   Design differences for communication between client and server processes
    2.9   What are the objectives and benefits of client/server?
    2.10   Overview of the techniques for client/server
    2.11   Impact of client/server on traditional techniques
    2.12   Introduction to the System Development Template
    2.13   Introduction to the three schema specification architecture (3–SSA)
    2.14   Client/Server applications in the context of the SDT and the 3–SSA
    2.15   Introduction to client/server physical design

3		**Project management**	**29**
	3.1	Introduction	
	3.2	Features of client/server design projects	
	3.3	User involvement	
	3.4	Quality procedures	
4		**Tailoring of the default SSADM structural model**	**33**
	4.1	SSADM modules and stages	
	4.2	Stage 0: Feasibility Study	
	4.3	Stage 1: Investigation of the Current Environment	
	4.4	Stage 2: Business System Options	
	4.5	Stage 3: Requirements Specification	
	4.6	Stage 4: Technical System Options	
	4.7	Stage 5: Logical Design	
	4.8	Stage 6: Physical Design	
5		**Product structure and descriptions**	**41**
	5.1	Introduction	
	5.2	Summary of product changes	
	5.3	SSADM, client/server and the SDT from a product point of view	
	5.4	Requirements Catalogue	
	5.5	Distribution Option	
	5.6	User Catalogue	
	5.7	Business Location Type	
	5.8	Workstation Type	
	5.9	Event Package	
	5.10	Enquiry Package	
	5.11	Entity Access Matrix	
	5.12	Technical System Architecture	
	5.13	Platform Description	
	5.14	Message Channel Description	
	5.15	Standard Mapping	
	5.16	Client/Server Design	
	5.17	Task Model	

6		**Techniques**	**71**
	6.1	Introduction	
	6.2	Summary of technique changes	
	6.3	SSADM, client/server and the SDT from a technique point of view	
	6.4	Requirements definition	
	6.5	Business area modelling	
	6.6	Entity-event modelling	
	6.7	Technical architecture definition	
	6.8	Client/Server partitioning	
	6.9	Client design	
	6.10	Server design	
	6.11	Technical system options	

Annex

A	Case study	101
	Bibliography	125
	Glossary	127
	Index	131

Chapter 1
Introduction

1 Introduction

1.1 Purpose of this volume

This volume has been written to explain in detail how SSADM can be used on projects to design client/server applications. This guidance is not a change of scope for SSADM. It simply shows how the concepts of client/server technology can be mapped to the method, particularly during Internal Design (refer to section 2.13).

The volume includes an overview explaining:

- what is meant by the term 'client/server'
- why the technology might be used
- the potential benefits
- why a distinct approach is necessary and the effects this has on the default SSADM project lifecycle.

The project management issues raised by the adoption of client/server technology are identified and discussed.

The information in this volume is compatible with the rationale and the method as published in the *SSADM Version 4 Reference Manual* and the *SSADM Version 4+ Manual*. It is consistent with the Information Systems Engineering Library volumes: *SSADM and GUI Design: A Project Manager's Guide* and *Distributed Systems: Application Development*.

1.2 Scope

This volume is concerned with the specification and design of the software necessary to support end-user applications. The volume addresses the expertise and methods appropriate for SSADM practitioners who must explore and document business requirements and design software that delivers services to end-users. The volume is not concerned with the expertise and methods needed by software engineers responsible for designing and constructing systems software and infrastructure components.

The products necessary to the design of a client/server application produced using SSADM are identified in this volume. Some of these products are specific to client/server technology, while others are extensions of

SSADM and Client/Server Applications

products already defined by the default SSADM method. This volume introduces the techniques required to develop new products, and necessary variations of the default SSADM techniques are explained.

The volume is targeted at practitioners working in environments where database management systems provide the technical support for client/server applications. It presupposes the use of appropriate tools and assumes that the technical services needed to support client/server applications are provided by a suitable software and hardware infrastructure.

This volume assumes that applications built with its guidance will not be targeted at environments using distributed databases, that is, environments that employ peer-to-peer communications, where the data is distributed and where its physical location is a major design consideration. For further advice on this topic, the reader should refer to the Information Systems Engineering Library volume: *Distributed Systems: Application Development*.

Client/Server technology is often associated with the use of graphical user interfaces (GUI). However, it is perfectly possible, although rarely the case, to construct client/server applications using human/computer interfaces that do not adhere to the WIMP (windows, icons, menus and pointers) paradigm. User interface interactions may be via character based screens and keyboards, and IT operations may be voice actuated or batch oriented. The client/server nature of an application is determined by its structural organization rather than by the interface perceived by the external world. It is expected that applications developed using this guidance will include both those using GUI technology and others. For more information on the use of SSADM with GUI, refer to the Information Systems Engineering Library volume: *SSADM and GUI Design: A Project Manager's Guide*.

| 1.3 | **Who should read this volume** | This volume is aimed primarily at IT managers, project managers and development staff who are considering or actively embarking on the design of software applications based on a client/server architecture. |

Chapter 1
Introduction

It is assumed that readers will be already familiar with SSADM Version 4.

The volume will be of interest to those investigating how to use client/server technology to fulfil business requirements for:

- portable applications
- usable applications that maximize end-user efficiency
- minimized operating costs
- minimized investment costs
- applications with high levels of reliability and availability.

1.4 Structure

This volume has six chapters.

Chapter 2 introduces:

- 'client/server' and defines it within the SSADM context
- some key issues for designers of client/server systems
- the potential benefits of using client/server technology
- the techniques required for development of client/server applications
- changes to familiar SSADM deliverables
- the Systems Development Template and the 3–schema specification architecture and details those changes necessary for a client/server environment
- necessary terminology, which is defined and explained.

Project management issues and responsibilities are discussed in Chapter 3.

Chapter 4 discuses the tailoring of the default SSADM structural model. Chapter 5 describes the products to be produced and their structure, and discusses the relationships between the products.

SSADM and Client/Server Applications

Chapter 6 describes the techniques used to originate the products discussed in Chapter 5. In Chapters 5 and 6, recommended changes are discussed first, then new products or techniques are introduced as appropriate.

1.5 Reader's guide

For those readers with limited time, who want to find quickly the sections most relevant to themselves, the following reading order is suggested.

IT managers and strategists

IT managers and strategists, responsible for setting policies and standards and choosing an organization-wide infrastructure should read:

- Chapter 2, Concepts
- Chapter 3, Project management.

Project managers

Project managers responsible for managing client/server projects should read:

- Chapter 2, Concepts
- Chapter 3, Project management
- Chapter 4, Tailoring of the default SSADM structural model
- Chapter 5, Product structure and descriptions.

SSADM practitioners

SSADM practitioners, actively involved with development of client/server systems, should read the entire volume.

Chapter 2
Concepts

2 Concepts

2.1 What is client/server?

A 'client' is a process that makes requests to another process (a 'server') and has the means to utilize that service. A server is a process that provides services on request for one or more clients.

Figure 2.1: Client/Server

One specific example of client/server (of many possible system layouts) is client personal computers, talking to a server (a database), on a host machine (as shown in Figure 2.1). We use the term 'host' for any machine managing resource for a group, department, division or whole organization. Banking details could be held on a database on the server and requests for information can be made from a remote client asking for a customer balance. The information would be displayed and possibly manipulated on the client, then sent back to the server for database update.

It is simplistic to think of clients only as PCs or workstations and servers as mainframes or mid-range machines. Client/Server describes a relationship between processes (software), not hardware. An important distinction is to think in terms of the role a machine performs as opposed to its size. For example, a mainframe process in the client role can invoke a server process running on a minicomputer. Similarly, a client application on a mid-range host can access a server on a workstation and a database server on a mainframe. It is a myth that clients are always small machines and servers are always large machines.

SSADM and Client/Server Applications

2.2 The client/server relationship can be hierarchic

Client/Server is an example of distributed processing; it involves an application with two or more processors.

The client process is active (it requests), the server process is reactive (it responds when asked). Requests are made by messages or remote procedure calls, the transmissions of which are usually carried by a network.

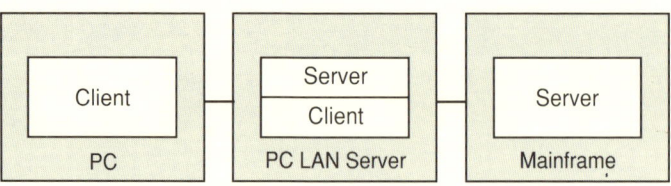

Hierarchic client/server relationship

Figure 2.2: Client/Server via a PC Local Area Network(LAN)

A machine can operate in many processing roles though not simultaneously. For example, it can operate as a server on a PC LAN, but also act as a client to another server on a mainframe as shown in Figure 2.2. This concept of layering of processes is important as is described later in this chapter.

2.3 Examples of clients and servers

A typical client/server application is supported by many client desktop machines running a frontend user-interface communicating with servers which perform routine tasks.

A server is often set-up on a dedicated machine configured for a specific type of service (for example file, facsimile, database, image, or communications). Most servers operate on machines with increased capabilities such as memory or processor power and additional reliability features such as un-interruptible power supplies, disk mirroring and fault tolerance, but some servers such as a print server will successfully run on a low specification machine.

2.4 A cross section of an application

Figure 2.3 shows an application perceived as containing:

- a user interface, a type of physical screen or hand held device that displays characters or graphics and

Chapter 2
Concepts

handles via presentation logic a user's interaction with the device (particularly input, edits and formatting)

- application function logic, where the business rules are applied

- data access logic, which delivers data to/from the application function and maintains integrity (such as security or completeness).

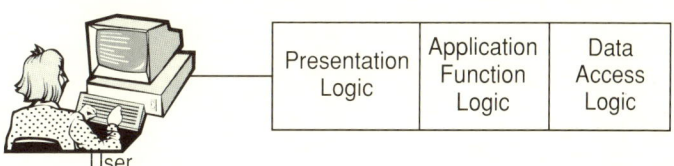

Figure 2.3: An application's logic components

Until recently the three pieces of a system, that is, the presentation, application and data access, typically ran on one local processor (for example a PC or a mainframe). With client/server technology a designer is able to distribute the software on to different processors (see Figure 2.4). The techniques of client/server partitioning, client design and server design support the process of distributed design.

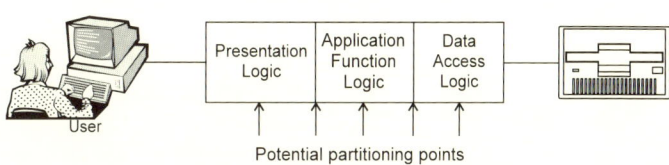

Figure 2.4: Client/Server partitioning

2.5 Key issues for designers of client/server systems

The key issues for designers are:

- where shall the application (presentation, application function and data access) be partitioned across multiple platforms?

15

SSADM and Client/Server Applications

- what processing roles (as clients and servers) should be assigned to each platform?
- how will the processes communicate?

2.6 Examples of client/server partitioning

There are many possible physical combinations of client/server partitioning. In this chapter we shall restrict ourselves to the three examples shown in Figures 2.5, 2.6 and 2.7.

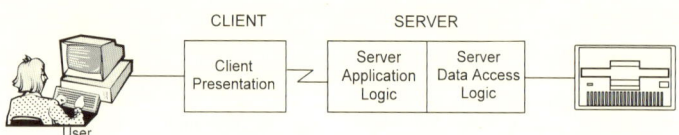

Figure 2.5: Server partitioned

A common example is where all of the presentation layer is relocated onto the client. The application and data remain on the server. Typically a GUI will be running on the client and a powerful DBMS will be running on the server as indicated in Figure 2.5.

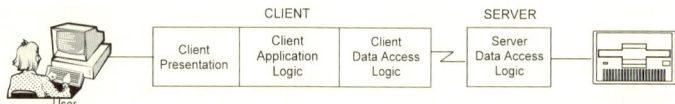

Figure 2.6: Client partitioned

A second example is distributed data access as in Figure 2.6. The client operates the bulk of the application. The server conducts file or database access. This example is one of the commonest partitioning approaches in client/server computing.

A third example is distributed application as shown in Figure 2.7. The application logic is partitioned and communicates via messages. This approach allows design and tuning flexibility, but is often unsuitable for the migration of legacy systems (where the code cannot be easily split).

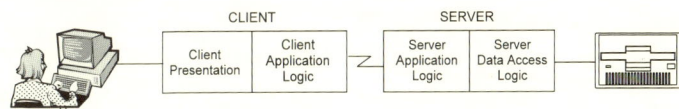

Figure 2.7: Both client and server partitioned

The correct choice of client/server partitioning is very closely related to the technical architecture adopted. Section 6.5 provides more details about technical architecture definition. In the 3–schema specification architecture diagrams at the beginning of both Chapters 5 and 6, technical architecture definition comes under policies and procedures. Therefore client/server partitioning is also related to this area of the 3–schema specification architecture.

More detailed explanations of client/server partitioning are available in Chapter 6, Techniques.

Table 2.1 gives an example of how a client/server application may be partitioned between the client and server components. Notice we have shown there can be distributed application logic on both client and server.

Example Client Services	Example Server Services
Presentation (graphical or character)	Print, facsimile, image
Terminal emulation	File, database, transaction
Local application logic, for example word processor	Communications
Distributed application logic	Distributed application logic
E–mail	E–mail
	Network management
	Resource management
	Configuration management
	Security

Table 2.1: Client/Server partitioning

2.7 Design differences for transaction processing

Client/Server applications process transactions. A transaction, often called a unit of work, is a component of business logic that is a sequential collection of one or more events and/or one or more enquiries which either updates all data/presentation components on a commit, or aborts leaving all components unchanged on a roll-back. If a transaction has been initiated but not committed, locks on the data will continue to be held until a commit or a roll-back arrives. As enquiries do not change any of the data components, they can be set up as small units of work to avoid holding locks on data. Many commercially available transaction management software products were designed for operation on one local processor and cannot accommodate client/server partitioning.

A client/server systems designer must consider the processing roles for the client, for the server, and for both a client and a server assigned to each platform.

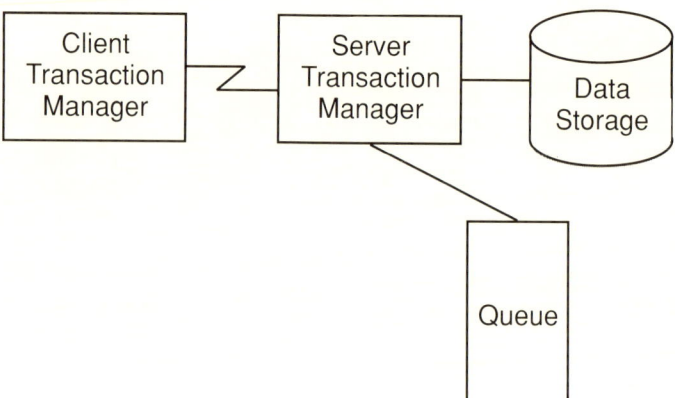

Figure 2.8: Remote transaction management

A more complex approach is remote transaction management as shown in Figure 2.8, where a transaction initiated from a client crosses the network and updates data on a remote server processor, such as a database server. In this example several data manipulation statements (requests) are combined into a transaction on a single database. A number of these transactions can be initiated from the client and managed in the form of a queue by the Server Transaction Manager.

Chapter 2
Concepts

Figure 2.9 shows a distributed transaction applying updates on multiple platforms. It is considerably more complex than local or remote transactions as the databases need to be kept consistent across a network. Data consistency is maintained by 'two-phase commit', where in phase 1 the databases are alerted to the update, then committed in phase 2 with a network-wide signal. There would need to be a requirement to protect against the failure of a node during a commit.

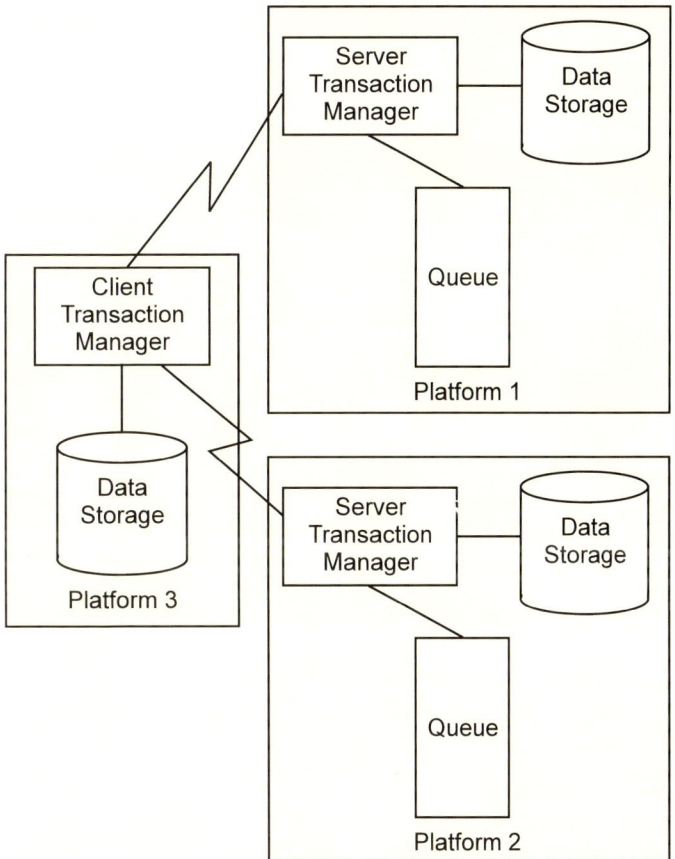

Figure 2.9: Distributed transaction

SSADM and Client/Server Applications

2.8 Design differences for communication between client and server processes

Remote procedure calls (a call from a client process to a server process on another machine) are in wide use on client/server systems. A remote procedure call is often more than just a subroutine CALL. For example, it can support automatic data conversion between different hardware and software platforms and authentication algorithms between client and server.

2.9 What are the objectives and benefits of client/server?

All innovations must offer specific benefits if they are to be widely adopted by business organizations. Client/Server technology is no exception. It offers a number of opportunities for:

- improving application usability
- reducing operating costs
- maximizing application flexibility
- reducing the dependency of remote locations upon centralized services
- separating the application issues from the technical architecture
- open technical environment, that is, a technical environment not tied to just one vendor or just a small number of vendors.

Improving application usability

Computer applications often impose large running costs on the businesses that own them. These include:

- effort spent by users entering and retrieving information
- effort spent training users
- time and effort expended by users in referring to manuals
- cost of repairing operator errors
- cost of rectifying mistakes that cause expense to customers
- business opportunities lost because users spend more time than necessary operating computer applications.

Although a client/server application does not have to have a sophisticated user interface, such an interface can be more effectively implemented by using a client/server architecture since the presentation logic can be kept distinct from business logic and the data access logic.

Client/Server provides enabling technology for improved usability of applications because of this partitioning capability. Users can participate in the prototyping of user interface standards which form the foundation of an easy to use, self explanatory system.

Reduced operating costs	The cost/power ratio of modern hardware creates an opportunity for business to downsize/rightsize its information systems infrastructure. The use of an open technical environment will reduce the cost of software components. Sophisticated, 4GL script languages and relational database management systems (RDBMS) are readily available for use on today's low cost, high power hardware.
Maximizing application flexibility	Client/Server technology maximizes ability to react to change with the least possible impact and cost by separating the user interface, required processing and business information as opposed to the restrictions of monolithic legacy systems. The business functions of a system can be developed where they are needed because client/server encourages these functions to be separate. Presentation, data access and business logic might very well be interleaved in monolithic legacy systems.
Reducing the dependency of remote locations upon centralized services	Remote business units can reduce their dependence on a central location, for instance, when communications fail, by using local processing and local data storage (either a replica of corporate data or distributed data). If a system has been downsized to facilitate the use of powerful PCs, the server(s) could be moved locally.
Separating the application issues from the technical architecture	It is possible to replace/upgrade the technical hardware components if the mapping between the logical architecture of an application and the infrastructure's technical architecture is clear.
Open technical environment	An open technical environment encourages choice of components from different vendors and reduces the need to purchase all components such as programming environment, RDBMS, configuration management tools

SSADM and Client/Server Applications

and CASE tools from a single supplier which is typical of the 4GL environment.

2.10 Overview of the techniques for client/server

There are four main techniques for development of client/server applications:

- defining the technical architecture
- client/server partitioning
- client design
- server design.

Defining the technical architecture

This technique involves the set-up and verification of standard components such as standard mapping guidelines (see Chapter 6) for partitioning the application into the chosen physical environment. The technical architecture should, wherever possible, be defined and verified by running a pilot project before conducting a client/server project.

Client/Server partitioning

This technique describes how to transform a client/server application specification into a physical design for a specific client/server architecture.

Client design

This technique describes the detailed design and development of the client software components. It supports the transformation from a prototype (GUI or character based) into a real production application.

Server design

This technique describes the detailed design and development of the server software components identified by mapping the specification into the physical architecture. It supports the design of:

- data oriented components such as stored procedures and triggers for maintenance of data integrity
- server application components, such as DBMS stored procedures, transaction processing (TP) modules and server processes invoked through remote procedure calls.

2.11 Impact of client/server on traditional techniques

Development of client/server applications requires a change of approach to established techniques in SSADM.

Chapter 2
Concepts

	User modelling	This technique builds on the 'standard' SSADM approach to defining user roles (for instance, an Accounts Clerk or a Human Resources Manager). For client/server design, there is greater scope to provide custom or tailorable user interfaces aligned to differing skills and capabilities as defined in the user roles. Users may be assigned to a variety of Business Location Types (to be discussed in Chapter 5), where they perform specific (and often subtly different) tasks at each location.
	Requirements Specification	The Requirements Specification needs greater emphasis on quantifying non-functional requirements within which there will be an early evaluation of critical technical requirements (described in more detail in section 5.4: Requirements Catalogue).
	Logical data modelling	This requires only slight change from 'standard' SSADM. When Business System Options are developed, the Logical Data Model must be able to support event identification. This permits initial analysis of distributed processing requirements.
2.12	Introduction to the System Development Template	SSADM concentrates primarily on the investigation of the business environment to define requirements and to specify the required system and the interface between that system and the external business world.

The System Development Template (SDT) can be used to show the relationships between the major SSADM products.

Figure 2.10 shows how the System Development Template illustrates the six areas of primary concern within a development:

- **investigation** of the business activities to be supported
- **specification** of the support required
- **construction**
- the **user environment**
- the **decision structure**
- organizational **policies and procedures**.

23

SSADM and Client/Server Applications

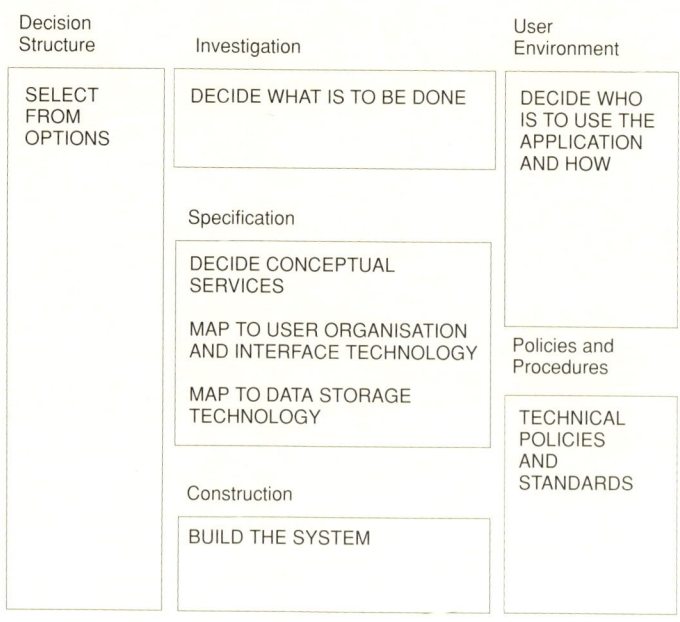

Figure 2.10: The System Development Template

2.13 Introduction to the three schema specification architecture (3-SSA)

Specification itself can be divided into three components. Hence in SSADM we refer to the 3–schema specification architecture (3–SSA). These three schemata are:

- the **Conceptual Model** of the services necessary to support the business

- a specification of an **External Design** of the conceptual services and their users

- the **Internal Design** that maps the Conceptual Model onto an implementation technology that provides the means of storing, updating and retrieving the data.

For the Conceptual Model it is possible, within fairly narrow boundaries, to talk in terms of a 'right' answer to some desired level of precision and currency. This answer is based on the required business entities, relationships, events, enquiries and the corresponding outputs as indicated in Figure 2.11.

Chapter 2
Concepts

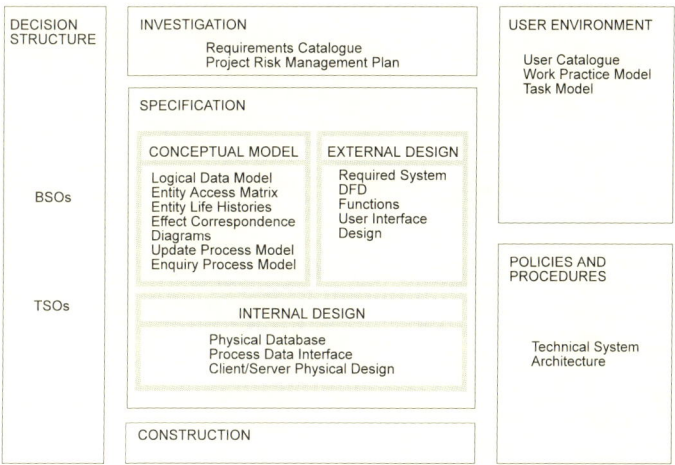

Figure 2.11: The 3-schema specification architecture

In contrast, there are many possible ways of designing the interface to the external user, just as there are many ways of implementing an application and many technologies available to help implement it.

2.14 **Client/Server applications in the context of the SDT and the 3-SSA**

Client/Server technology is just one means of implementing the IT support required by a business. As for any other technology, it is possible to map the deliverables produced in specifying and designing a client/server application to the System Development Template and the 3–schema specification architecture.

The 3–schema specification architecture advises a layered logical design.

The top layer of Figure 2.12 consists of the user interface derived from External Design. The middle layer represents the set of required services, expressed in terms of the events needed to keep the application data up-to-date and the enquiries and corresponding outputs by which information is extracted from the application. These are derived from the Conceptual Model. The foundation layer is the data itself, the entity types and their relationships derived from the Conceptual Model and Internal Design. In designing for client/server technology, designers are recommended to preserve this layering through into the physical design. This will maximize the maintainability of the application.

Figure 2.12: Layered logical design

This concept, of a layered architecture, is not peculiar to SSADM or to client/server applications.

2.15 Introduction to client/server physical design

Client/Server physical design (see Figure 2.13 for the mapping of physical design to layered logical design) is supported by three techniques: client/server partitioning, client design and server design.

Client/Server partitioning was mentioned in section 2.10 and will be described more fully in Chapter 6.

Client design (introduced in section 2.10 and detailed further in Chapter 6) deals with the detailed design and development of the client software components; for example, the client presentation layer may be coded in the GUI 4GL script and the client application layer may be in C language, Dynamic Linked Libraries and/or other 3GL code. Typically, the user interface is mapped on to the PC or workstation executing a GUI and/or a 4GL environment.

Chapter 2
Concepts

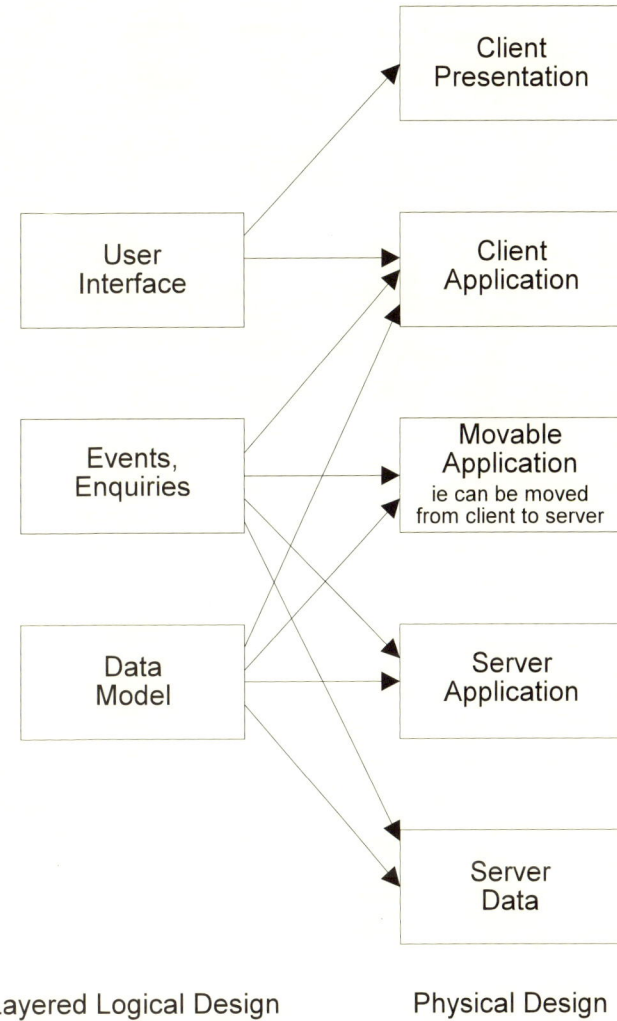

Figure 2.13: Layered logical design mapped to Physical Design

Server design (introduced in section 2.10 and detailed further in Chapter 6) deals with the detailed design and development of the server software components, such as the definition of declarative Physical Data Design integrity procedures and triggers, any server processes invoked through remote procedure calls. The data model (entity types and relationships) are typically mapped to a server running a relational database management system.

The server data layer will typically implement the RDBMS tables and referential integrity rules and may implement stored procedures and triggers. The server application layer is sometimes inside the RDBMS. If the RDBMS is unable to support stored procedures and triggers, the data constraints will need to be enforced in a server application layer outside the RDBMS.

Event and enquiry processing can be mapped wholly or partly to either a PC or workstation (client application layer) or the server application layer.

For more information on the physical design possibilities please refer to Chapter 6, Techniques.

It is also possible for the data model to be distributed across a number of servers. This is in the realm of distributed systems which is outside the scope of this volume. Please refer to the Information Systems Engineering Library volume *Distributed Systems: Application Development* for more information.

3 Project management

3.1 Introduction

The objective of a project manager is to deliver a quality product that satisfies an agreed set of prioritized functional and non-functional requirements, and that is delivered to budget, on time, using the resources available.

The current novelty of client/server technology increases the problems for all those involved in the management of a project. However, the stability provided by a tried and trusted method such as SSADM, particularly when used in conjunction with the PRINCE project management method, should enable an experienced project manager to tackle those problems in a manner that reduces risk to a minimum.

This chapter sets out to highlight those areas where managers need to understand the impact of client/server. The guidance is intended as a supplement to current SSADM and PRINCE, not to replace them. Much of what follows reflects good practice equally applicable to a wide variety of projects.

3.2 Features of client/server design projects

The key difference between a client/server application and a traditional implementation is generally the requirement to deliver an application on a set of interoperating components each running on a separate platform. The task of delivering a reliable system in multiple environments as opposed to in a single environment is obviously made harder the more platforms that are involved.

Each component of a client/server system must be of sufficiently high quality to ensure that the combination of these components achieves a satisfactory level of reliability. Hence, projects adopting client/server technology must pay considerable heed to quality assurance and requirements for software reliability, fault tolerance, robustness and the ability to adapt to technological change.

The client/server nature of the applications discussed in this volume necessitates and enables the separate

SSADM and Client/Server Applications

specification, development and testing of the various software components needed for such an application. A key task for the project manager is, therefore, to divide project resources and to ensure that inter-developer communication problems are minimized by early and rigorous definition of the interfaces between components.

One aspect of change that merits particular note, is that it may be necessary to make technical decisions regarding the hardware and software infrastructure much earlier than usual. Indeed, it is often necessary to develop an application to work in a co-operative environment alongside other extant applications. The choice of operating environment may be made at a strategic level within the business organization. It may impose requirements and constraints on the application design.

3.3 User involvement

Understanding users' needs and how they perceive those needs is fundamental to the success of a client/server project as with all projects, and there is a need for effective user involvement throughout the project life-cycle. Often, this is best achieved by including user representatives in the development team. They can then contribute directly to the identification, specification and quantification of the critical requirements and help with monitoring and testing the capabilities of the end products.

Client/Server developments, particularly when based on GUI technology, will often make use of prototyping techniques in order to define user interfaces and standards. In the use of such techniques, there is much day to day contact between users and developers, and joint effort is seen to be directed toward a common goal. This increased user involvement brings many benefits but also can be the source of delay and fruitless iteration. Project managers must be careful to ensure that the ability to prototype and the need to fulfil quality constraints do not lead to over-engineering or a focus upon one requirement at the expense of others. Establishing tolerance levels for non-functional requirements, and prioritizing functional requirements, helps developers to avoid expensive overengineering,

Chapter 3
Project management

while setting measurable targets avoids under-engineering.

3.4 Quality procedures

As mentioned earlier in this chapter, project managers must pay particular attention to quality assurance and requirements for software reliability, fault tolerance and robustness when adopting client/server technology.

The potential for employing a number of diverse technologies and platforms within a client/server development means that a project manager must define clear and measurable targets for all aspects of the design. The non-functional requirements must be given quality criteria that are quantifiable and consistent.

Coupled with this is the probability of dealing with multiple vendors in the supply and support of the different platforms and technologies. It is important that the project manager can produce an agreed approach to problem solving with these vendors.

It is the role of the project manager to manage the risk of the project for the following purposes:

- to identify the threats to a project's ability to deliver a desired product that fully meets all the functional and non-functional requirements, to budget and on time

- to plan and initiate counter actions that avoid, transfer or reduce a project's exposure to the threats, and to manage the impact of threats when they materialize.

SSADM and Client/Server Applications

4 Tailoring of the default SSADM structural model

| 4.1 | SSADM modules and stages

This chapter shows how the steps within each stage of core SSADM changes for client/server considerations. The only stage that changes significantly is Stage 4 Technical System Options, which includes two additional steps.

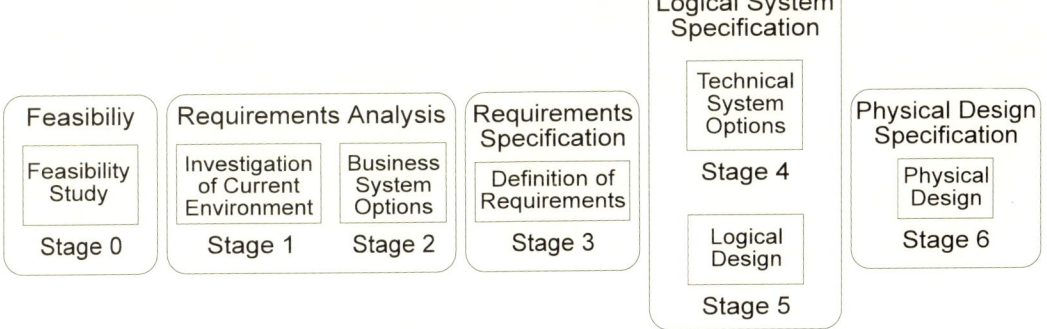

Figure 4.1: SSADM Modules and Stages

| 4.2 | Stage 0: Feasibility Study

No structural change to the Feasibility Module is necessary. Some changes are needed in the detail of steps.

Step 010: Prepare for Feasibility Study

The Product Initiation Document (PID) should indicate why client/server technology is considered suitable. In particular, it should indicate if there are non-functional requirements that are critical to the project's success. For instance:

- stability of design (the ability to add new clients with minimum effect on the processing and database architecture)

- maximum usability for a variety of users with widely differing perceptions of the business

- portability and protection against technological change.

The PID should state if solutions other than client/server are acceptable.

SSADM and Client/Server Applications

	Step 020: Define the Problem	The Requirements Catalogue is extended to include non-functional requirements for all those dimensions of the project that are critical to success (see requirements definition in Chapter 6).
	Step 030: Select Feasibility Options	The feasibility study must concentrate on defining the project scope as unambiguously as possible, in terms of functional and non-functional requirements. Preferably non-functional requirements should be quantified so achievement in all the critical dimensions can be tested and success or failure demonstrated. However, usually we must be content to identify the critical dimensions, as the resources allocated to the feasibility study are usually insufficient to permit a high level of detail. It must be postponed until Stage 3 Requirements Specification.
	Step 040: Assemble Feasibility Report	The procedure is unchanged. The Feasibility Report must address client/server requirements in addition to the contents described in core SSADM.
4.3	**Stage 1: Investigation of the Current Environment**	No structural change to Stage 1 is necessary. Some changes are required in the detail of steps.
	Step 110: Establish Analysis Framework	As for the feasibility study, project input documentation should describe the geography of the organisation and must say why there is a requirement for client/server which may be based on: • non-function requirements (based on factors such as performance, data integrity and data quality) • cost • stability of design (the ability to add new clients with minimum effect on the processing and database architecture). Planned project activities, end-product definitions and plans for the involvement of users must all take account of client/server issues.
	Step 120: Investigate and Define Requirements	Requirements must address the needs for robustness and consistency. For example, what contingency measures should be taken during system down time or communication failures.

Chapter 4
Tailoring of the default SSADM structural model

		Types of business location must be defined and cross-referenced to requirements. A requirement may serve more than one Business Location Type (see Chapter 5).
	Step 130: Investigate Current Processing	The procedure is unchanged.
	Step 140: Investigate Current Data	The procedure is unchanged. The Logical Data Model (LDM) is developed as a single model for the entire system.
	Step 150: Derive Logical View of Current Services	This procedure is unchanged.
	Step 160: Assemble Investigation Results	This procedure is unchanged.
4.4	**Stage 2: Business System Options**	No structural change to Stage 2 is necessary.
	Step 210: Define Business System Options	This procedure is unchanged.
	Step 220: Select Business System Option	This procedure is unchanged.
4.5	**Stage 3: Requirements Specification**	There is no need for structural change to Requirements Specification, although some additions are necessary in the detail of steps.
	Step 310: Define Required System Processing	The following changes are needed to the procedure in this step: • as in core SSADM, requirements definition (see Chapter 6) is an iterative technique where the Requirements Catalogue may be referenced, checked and updated at any time. The fulfillment of non-functional requirements (Chapter 5) is critical to the success of an application. Non-functional criteria need to be set during the initial analysis stage of a development

SSADM and Client/Server Applications

> • business area modelling (described in Chapter 6) needs to be performed here. Its purpose is to understand the relevant characteristics of the various populations of application users and the tasks performed by these users. This understanding provides a source for requirements, Business Location Types (Chapter 5), and Workstation Types (Chapter 5).

Step 320: Develop Required Data Model	This procedure is unchanged except that for client/server applications, the first cut creation of Enquiry Access Paths can be performed here but are refined as part of the extended entity-event modelling technique in Step 360.
Step 330: Derive System Functions	This procedure is largely unchanged, except that an initial idea of whether a function is client or server based should be documented. Further, I/O Structures are not applicable for the development of GUI client/server systems.
Step 340: Enhance Required Data Model	This procedure is unchanged.
Step 350: Develop Specification Prototypes	This procedure is unchanged.
Step 360: Develop Processing Specification	No change is needed in the procedure in this step. The entity-event modelling technique (refer to Chapter 6) used in this step is extended to include enquiries on the Event/Entity Matrix and is renamed the Entity Access Matrix. Effect Correspondence Diagrams are created as part of the Event Packages work. The Enquiry Package work updates the Enquiry Access Paths created earlier in Step 320.
	New functional requirements have been mapped to events and enquiries. At this stage, the scope, input and output of the events and enquiries should be well understood. Operations can be added to ECDs, EAPs and Entity Life Histories thereby reducing the effort required in process modelling in Stage 6.

Chapter 4
Tailoring of the default SSADM structural model

Step 370: Confirm System Objectives — This procedure is unchanged.

Step 380: Assemble Requirements Specification — This procedure is unchanged.

4.6 Stage 4: Technical System Options

Some structural change is required for the Technical System Options Stage with the addition of two steps (see Figure 4.2). The definition and selection of Distribution Options needs to be included. Some changes are also necessary in the detail of steps.

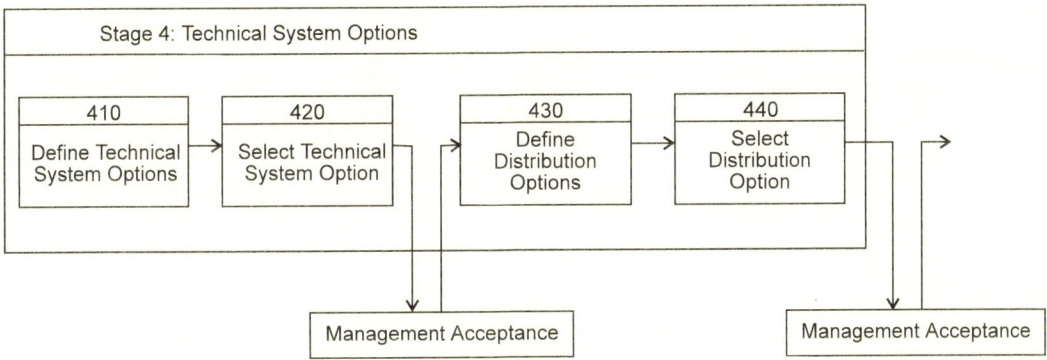

Figure 4.2: Additions to Technical System Options

Step 410: Define Technical System Options — This procedure is generally the same as in core SSADM, the creation of options has to take account of the technical architecture and therefore technical architecture definition (see Chapter 6) needs to be performed here. The Technical System Architecture (see Chapter 5) replaces the Technical Environment Description in this stage.

Technical architecture definition will use cross-reference information concerning events/enquiries, Business Location Types and volumetrics in order to determine the Standard Mapping (Chapter 5) and the required Platform Description and Message Channel Definition (Chapter 5).

SSADM and Client/Server Applications

	Step 420: Select Technical System Options	The objective is to describe a stable and robust model of optimum technical architecture for the application.
	Step 430: Define Distribution Options	The purpose of this new step is to present alternative approaches to the distribution of system functionality (expressed as events and enquiries) across the available system platforms arrived at from the technical architecture definition (see Distribution Option in Chapter 5).
	Step 440: Select Distribution Option	Certain quality criteria have to be met by a particular Distribution Option once it has been selected. Refer to Chapter 5 for full details.
4.7	**Stage 5: Logical Design**	No structural change is needed for this stage.
	Step 510: Design User Dialogues	This step may be unchanged if core dialogue design is necessary. However, since most client/server systems are GUI based, which is not relevant to core SSADM dialogue design, this step can be replaced with extended prototyping.
	Step 520: Define Update Processing	This procedure is unchanged, but should be extended to cover an initial first-cut logical view of:

- notification scheme
- integrity constraints
- triggers.

These are described in more detail in Chapter 6.

The approach taken will depend further on the choice of technical architecture made in Stage 4.

This step can be considered redundant if the Event and Enquiry Packages have been well enough defined to describe fully the processing required, and especially if ECDs have been extended to include operations. The operation lists are more appropriate to particular types of 4GL.

Step 530: Define Enquiry Processing — This procedure is unchanged but extended to cover the same issues as for defining update processing.

Chapter 4
Tailoring of the default SSADM structural model

Step 540: Assemble Logical Design	This procedure is unchanged.

4.8 Stage 6: Physical Design

Structurally, Stage 6 has not changed, but there is some difference in the approach taken in some of the steps.

Step 610: Prepare for Physical Design	This procedure is unchanged.
Step 620: Create Physical Data Design	This procedure is extended to facilitate server design (see Chapter 6). Server design provides a precise specification of the data and functionality at the server level.
Step 630: Create Function Component Implementation Map (FCIM)	This procedure is replaced by both client design and server design (see Chapter 6). The product of these is Client/Server Design (see Chapter 5) which is an enhancement of the Standard Mapping (see Chapter 5), part of Step 410.

For example, the Standard Mapping shows how an LDM maps into a DBMS like ORACLE DRS, how an interface object like MS Windows maps into MS Visual Basic Client Presentation.

The Client/Server Design describes this mapping in greater detail by showing what platform component each element of the LDM maps into (for example, Entity 1 maps to an ORACLE table and Entity 2 maps to a file on the client).

Some parts of Step 630 will still need to be retained like:
- identifying common processes
- removal of duplication
- success units
- syntax error handling
- physical I/O formats.

Additional note should also be made of the following:
- notification scheme
- integrity constraints
- triggers

SSADM and Client/Server Applications

- physical dialogues that will be dependent on technical architecture, especially GUI.

Step 640: Optimise Physical Data Design — This procedure remains unchanged but particular reference should be made to optimising for performance (within the scope of this document) on both the client and the server (see client design and server design in Chapter 6).

Step 650: Complete Function Specification — This procedure refers to Function Component Implementation Map (FCIM) which has been replaced by Client/Server Design (see Chapter 5). Therefore this step is only undertaken on the components of Client/Server Design that cannot be specified non-procedurally.

Step 660: Consolidate Process Data Interface — This procedure is extended to include an iterative validation of the client/server partitioning (performed as part of technical architecture definition in Stage 4) against the Client/Server Design derived in Step 630.

Step 670: Validate Physical Design — This procedure is unchanged.

Chapter 5
Product structure and descriptions

5 Product structure and descriptions

5.1 Introduction

The design of client/server applications necessitates the extension or formalization of some existing SSADM products and the addition of new products. However, the change to core SSADM is limited and is focused primarily on the physical design issues necessary to cope with the richer technical architectures commonly used in client/server applications.

This chapter is introduced via the System Development Template and details only those products that have been extended, altered or added to SSADM. In addition, notes are provided concerning those products which, although not altered by this volume, may require special consideration as to their most effective use in a client/server environment.

5.2 Summary of product changes

This section lists the new, altered and extended products.

The new products are:

- Business Location Type (see section 5.7)
- Client/Server Design (see section 5.16)
- Distribution Option (see section 5.5)
- Message Channel Definition (see section 5.14)
- Platform Description (see section 5.13)
- Standard Mapping (see section 5.15)
- Task Model (see section 5.17)
- Technical System Architecture (see section 5.12)
- Workstation Type (see section 5.8).

The altered, extended, and repackaged products are:

- Enquiry Package, a formalisation and extension of enquiries and the Enquiry Access Path (see section 5.10)
- Event Access Matrix, an extension of the Event/Entity Matrix (see section 5.11)

- Event Package, a formalisation and extension of events and the Effect Correspondence Diagram (see section 5.9)
- Requirements Catalogue (see section 5.4)
- User Catalogue (see section 5.6).

The replaced products are:

- DBMS Performance Classification, replaced by Platform Description
- DBMS Storage Classification, replaced by Platform Description
- Function Component Implementation Map, replaced by Client/Server Design
- Physical Environment Classification, replaced by Technical System Architecture
- Processing System Classification, replaced by Platform Description
- Technical Environment Description, replaced by Technical System Architecture.

5.3	SSADM, client/server and the SDT from a product point of view	Figure 5.1 shows the System Development Template (SDT) and embedded 3–schema specification architecture (3–SSA) structure of the major products required for SSADM and client/server.
5.4	Requirements Catalogue	This product is an extension of the Requirements Catalogue as defined in the *SSADM Version 4 Reference Manual*.
5.4.1	Purpose	To package details of all demands imposed on the system. At any time, the Requirements Catalogue is the repository for all known requirements.
		Client/Server applications require extension of the Requirements Catalogue. Functional requirements are documented as in core SSADM. However, a more rigorous approach to the non-functional requirements is needed.

Chapter 5
Product structure and descriptions

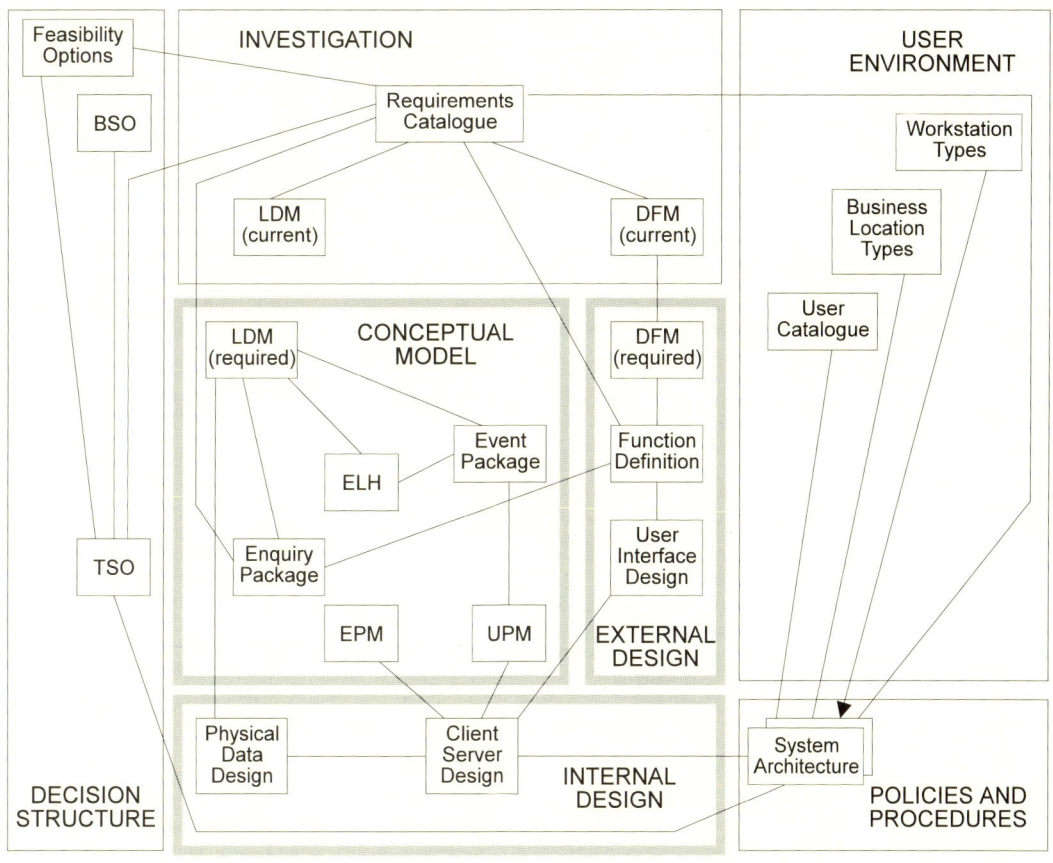

Figure 5.1: SDT and embedded 3-SSA from a product point of view

Client/Server systems are characterised by the increased importance of non-functional requirements, such as performance, data integrity and data quality. Within the set of non-functional requirements there will be a subset that place major constraints or demands on the technical infrastructure of the system, such as memory consuming applications storing large complex data structures. These are categorised within the extended Requirements Catalogue as an indicator within the critical technical requirements field. In organisations where the Technical System Architecture is established at a strategic level, the critical technical requirements are used to evaluate the feasibility of the project. In cases where the project team is at liberty to specify the Technical System Architecture, the critical technical requirements help the team to evaluate and select the most appropriate system infrastructure.

5.4.2 Composition

The Requirements Catalogue is formed in the same way as that used in core SSADM except in the case of non-functional requirements. These non-functional requirements are defined in this volume as comprising:

- a Non-functional Requirement Structure
- Non-functional Requirement Descriptions.

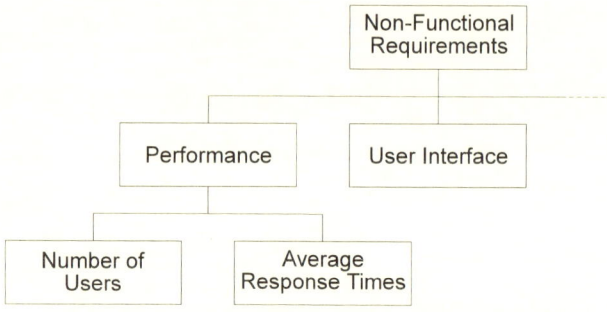

Figure 5.2: The Non-functional Requirement Structure

Non–functional Requirement Structure

The Non-functional Requirement Structure shown in Figure 5.2 is a hierarchic SSADM Structure Diagram. The normal topological rules of structure diagrams apply, but iteration and selection are not specified. Each branch of the Non-functional Requirement Structure is decomposed into two or more subrequirements, that can themselves be decomposed until the component subrequirements can be specified in measurable terms.

The hardware and software infrastructure upon which the required application will execute must be capable of supporting the application and delivering adequate performance in all the dimensions specified by the Non-functional Requirement Structure. The critical technical requirements summarise the global characteristics that the chosen Technical System Architecture must satisfy.

Chapter 5
Product structure and descriptions

Non-functional Requirement Description

An example of a Non-functional Requirement Description is shown in Table 5.1. Each leaf node on the Non-functional Requirement Structure should be numbered to create an identifier.

ID	NFR027	Critical?	Y / N
Description	There shall be no window action for which the average response time is more than 5 seconds.		
Quality Attribute	Typical response time		
Scale (for Quality Attribute)	Seconds		
Test for Achievement	Response times must be recorded for all actions in a variety of realistic user situations based on the required system usage.		
Target Level	5 seconds		
Tolerances	All actions should respond within 15 seconds.		
Cost of Missing Target Level	The cost of a 1-second degradation in performance has been calculated at approximately £2000		
Minimum Cost to achieve Target	Not yet known.		
References	NFR013 on system usage.		

Table 5.1: Non-functional Requirement Description

A Non-functional Requirement Description consists of:
- identifier/name
- indicator denoting a critical technical requirement (Y/N)
- textual description

45

- quality attribute concerned (such as typical response time, transaction throughput, reliability, availability, interoperability or conformance to standards)
- a scale of measure
- a test by which the achieved level can be monitored
- a target level
- high and low tolerance levels, which may take zero or infinity as acceptable values, if the requirement is to minimise or maximise the quality attribute
- the notional cost of missing the target level by one scale unit
- the minimum cost incurred if the target level of the non-functional requirement is achieved
- references to:
  - pertinent standards
  - other applications with which the application must interoperate.

5.4.3 Derivation

As described in the *SSADM Version 4 Reference Manual* and also the following:

- User Catalogue
- Task Model.

5.4.4 Quality criteria

For all requirements:

1 is the description of each requirement as complete as possible?

2 have source, owner, priority and benefit been identified?

3 if this requirement was previously defined, is the new version consistent with the old? If not, why not?

4 does the Requirements Catalogue describe all identified requirements of the new system (with any appropriate cross-references to other SSADM products)?

5 are requirements consistent with the project objectives?

Chapter 5
Product structure and descriptions

6 have all necessary previous requirements been carried forward?

For non-functional requirements:

1 does the NFR Structure conform to the topological rules of SSADM Structure Diagrams?

2 has every pertinent dimension of quality been considered (for example, see the ISO 9126 standard *Software Product Evaluation: Quality Characteristics and Guidelines for their Use*)?

3 is the Requirements Catalogue complete and consistent?

4 are all mandatory sections components complete (such as: textual description, scale of measure, target level and quality attribute)?

5 have critical technical requirements been identified?

5.4.5 External dependencies

Requirements are discussed and reviewed by the relevant users.

5.5 Distribution Option

This product is an addition to the SSADM Version 4 product set and forms part of Business System Options of the Decision Structure of the method (within the System Development Template).

5.5.1 Purpose

The purpose is to present alternative approaches to the distribution of system functionality (expressed as events and enquiries) across the available system platforms (see Figure 5.5 in section 5.15). The formulation and evaluation of Distribution Options will assist in the identification of a robust system topology that meets the non-functional requirements of the system.

Distribution Options are based on the chosen Technical System Architecture (defined in section 5.12) that supports applications in several projects.

The Distribution Options must be expressed in such a way as to allow the executive sponsors of the project (with the appropriate amount of technical consultation) to decide upon the most desirable distribution approach.

5.5.2 Composition

The Distribution Option product, though largely comprised of textual components, may be supplemented by a detailed picture/system structure diagram as shown in Figure 5.3.

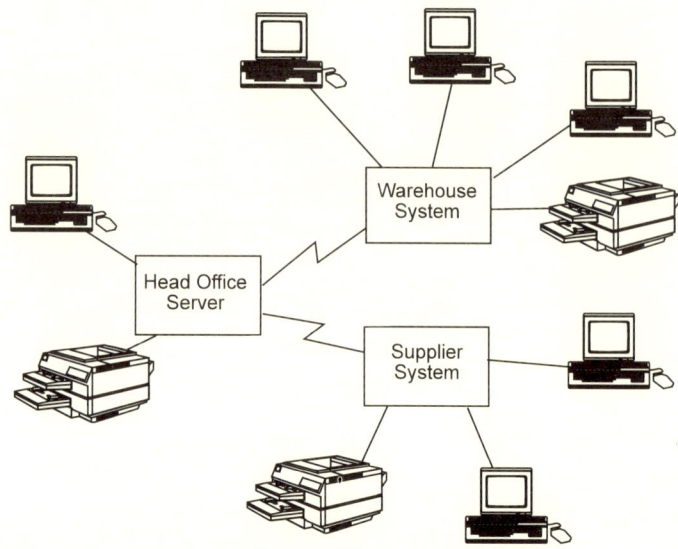

Figure 5.3: An example of a Distribution Option

The following information needs to be recorded about a Distribution Option:

- a textual description

- a platform/conceptual schema element cross-reference. Each platform will be identified together with the elements of the logical system (for example the Logical Data Model, user interface, events and enquiries) that will be implemented on it

- a business location impact analysis. For each Business Location Type (see section 5.7), two fields need to be completed:
    - a positive/negative indicator. A significant positive or negative impact may occur to the Business Location Type if the proposed option is adopted. For example, an event like 'Create New Order' might best or more efficiently emanate from one business location rather than another
    - an impact description

Chapter 5
Product structure and descriptions

- an integrity impact analysis. A list of integrity problems and inconsistencies that can occur, in different situations, if the Distribution Option is adopted, such as incomplete data emanating from one location

- project estimates. An indication of cost, effort, duration, skills and resource requirements and other relevant information. These figures may be derived through the application of Mark II Function Point Analysis although other methods will also be appropriate.

5.5.3	Derivation	The derivation of the Distribution Option product is from:

- Feasibility Report
- Requirements Catalogue
- Business System Options
- Technical System Architecture
- Processing Specification (particularly events, enquiries and Logical Data Model).

5.5.4	Quality criteria	The quality criteria are:

1. is the system definition consistent with the technical direction outlined in the Feasibility Report, the Selected Business System Option or both?
2. are all of the critical technical requirements satisfied?
3. is the option feasible within the confines of the project constraints?
4. is the option consistent with installation standards?
5. has the impact of the option on each Business Location Type been fully investigated?

5.5.5	External dependencies	Confirmation of technical feasibility and practicality will be required from in-house or external experts.
5.6	**User Catalogue**	This product is an extension of the User Catalogue as defined in the *SSADM Version 4 Reference Manual*.

SSADM and Client/Server Applications

The User Catalogue needed for client/server design is an extension of the core SSADM User Catalogue. Rather than simply listing the individuals who interact on-line with a system, it is concerned with distinguishing the many classes of user, the kinds of geographic site from which they operate and hence the business activities that must be supported at the various kinds of business location. The product subsumes the existing User Catalogue.

The extension of the User Catalogue is a mandatory step for the completion of a successful client/server development, its creation will enhance the understanding of non-functional requirements, Business Location Types and workstation requirements.

5.6.1 Purpose

The purpose of the User Catalogue is to document the characteristics of the various populations of application user. This information is needed as an input to Requirements Specification, in order to determine the functional and non-functional requirements imposed by the users and as a precursor to the definition of SSADM functions.

Different user populations perform a variety of business activities. Individual users may perform some activities in common with other users, but may have particular responsibility for specific activities. In order to provide suitable IT support for all the business activities carried out by particular users, there is a need to identify and document these user classes (for example, a manager, a reviewer or a worker). These often exhibit many to many relationships with the job titles with which an organization labels its staff. This complexity needs to be unravelled and understood.

5.6.2 Composition

The composition of the User Catalogue product is:

- a set of User Definitions each with:
  - a job title
  - multiple, textual, job activity descriptions or references to a set of user tasks defined in a Task Model
  - a user/user class cross-reference
- a set of user class definitions each with:

- a user class name
- type of access to the application (such as direct, indirect, remote or for support)
- frequency of application access
- mandatory/optional use (of the systems)
- use of other applications, especially if there is a need for applications to interoperate
- number of individual users of this type

- a user class/task, user class/Data Flow Model process or user class/function cross-reference defining what users of the class do

- a user class/user definition cross-reference

- a user class/Business Location Type cross-reference defining where users work

- a user class/Workstation Type cross-reference defining what the users will work on.

5.6.3 Derivation

The derivation of the User Catalogue product is from:

- Project Initiation Document
- discussions with users
- Requirements Catalogue
- Context Diagram
- Current Physical Data Flow Model
- Overview Logical Data Model
- Task Model.

5.6.4 Quality criteria

The quality criteria are:

1 are all classes of user identified?

2 is the entire user population represented in one of the user definitions and one of the user classes?

3 are all the tasks (from the Task Model) that are relevant to this class of user identified?

4 have the User Roles performed by staff with all the relevant job titles been investigated?

5 have the user classes been defined at the correct level of granularity (for example user classes that encompassed too many Business Location Types or

SSADM and Client/Server Applications

user definitions could lead to a reduction of its effectiveness)?

6 are the sets of user definitions and user classes complete and consistent?

5.6.5	External dependencies	Relevant users to review their entries in the User Catalogue.
5.7	**Business Location Type**	This product is an addition to the SSADM Version 4 product set and forms part of the method's user environment (within the System Development Template).
5.7.1	Purpose	User populations are assigned to geographically distinct sites where particular subsets of business activity are performed. When developing client/server systems, the SSADM practitioner needs information regarding the various kinds of site (including for example, offices, shops, warehouses or garages) and the subsets of activity that will be hosted at each. This information is necessary to enable the development of a human/computer interface and functionality for the user population within a level of service appropriate to the business locations.
		Hence, Business Location Types are defined and cross-referenced with the definitions of user classes within the User Catalogue.
5.7.2	Composition	A business location is a specific site where business activities take place. Moreover, business locations are locations from which functions (processes from Internal Design) may be triggered. Various business sites may be exactly similar in the kinds of business activities that are performed there. They may be occupied by users of similar user classes and hence the IT support required may be the same at one site as at another. In this case, they are regarded as the same Business Location Type. For each such, there is a need to document:

- identifier/name
- textual description
- number of business locations of this type
- a Business Location Type/task, Business Location Type/Data Flow Model process or Business Location Type/function cross-reference

Chapter 5
Product structure and descriptions

- a Business Location Type/user class cross-reference
- a Business Location Type/Workstation Type cross-reference. Each business location needs to be supplied with Workstations that users may use in the pursuance of their User Roles. Hence, for each Business Location Type a set of Workstation Requirements can be determined by means of this cross-reference.

5.7.3 Derivation

The derivation of the Business Location Type product is from:

- Project Initiation Document
- discussions with users
- Requirements Catalogue
- Context Diagram
- Current Physical Data Flow Model
- Overview Logical Data Model
- Task Model.

5.7.4 Quality criteria

The quality criteria are:

1. has each business location been accommodated within one of the Business Location Types?
2. are the set of Business Location Types, Workstation Types and user classes consistent?

5.7.5 External dependencies

Business Location Types are discussed and reviewed with relevant users.

5.8 Workstation Type

This product is an addition to the SSADM Version 4 product set and forms part of the method's User Environment Model (within the System Development Template).

5.8.1 Purpose

Individual users, depending on their user classes, impose a variety of demands on the components of the application with which they interact, particularly their workstations. Some users impose high demands on workstations – for example, desktop publishers, graphic designers and multi-media artists require support for a wide range of drawing and document layout functions at

SSADM and Client/Server Applications

terminals with large display areas, fast screen refresh rates, special input and output devices (such as mice, graphics tablets, the capability to capture and play video images and audio tracks).

The designers and implementors need to know the capabilities of the various kinds of workstations required and how those workstations need to be distributed between the different Business Location Types. Otherwise time may be spent over or under engineering certain parts of the system that could otherwise be overcome by a using a particular type of workstation.

5.8.2 Composition

For each Workstation Type there is needed:

- a name/identifier
- a textual description
- specialist use (for example, multi-media)
- a Workstation Type/Business Location cross-reference.

5.8.3 Derivation

The derivation of the Workstation Type product is from:

- Project Initiation Document
- discussions with users
- Requirements Catalogue
- Context Diagram
- Current Physical Data Flow Model
- Overview Logical Data Model
- Task Model.

5.8.4 Quality criteria

The quality criteria are:

1 have all user workstations and terminals been accommodated within one of the Workstation Types?

2 is the set of Workstation Types, Business Location Types and user classes consistent?

5.8.5 External dependencies

There may be a requirement for external expertise on particular specialized workstation types.

Chapter 5
Product structure and descriptions

5.9 Event Package This product is an aggregation and extension of the events (identified as part of Function Definition) and Effect Correspondence Diagrams (produced using entity-event modelling) as defined in the *SSADM Version 4 Reference Manual*.

5.9.1 Purpose The purpose is to define the events that initiate system processing and document the way in which these events effect the data of the system. This aggregation is a standard requirement of SSADM Version 4 but is extended to provide additional information of importance in client/server developments. Thus, the Event Package is extended to provide a cross-reference to the Business Location Types from which they originate, their mode of operation (for example, critical on-line) and their detailed volumetrics (such as the daily volume for each Business Location Type).

Note that as events emanate from functions as defined in core SSADM, any mode of operation attached to an event is automatically attached to the function: that is, if the event is critical on-line, so must be the function.

The Event Package will be taken forward into Logical System Specification and Physical Design as the encapsulation of system processing and will provide a full logical definition of the elements of system functionality that must be supported by the new client/server system.

5.9.2 Composition The Event Package consists of an event definition and an Effect Correspondence Diagram.

Event definition The event definition (see Table 5.2) is as follows:
- function name/identifier
- event name/identifier
- mode (such as batch, on-line, critical on-line)
- description
- frequency (per day)

55

SSADM and Client/Server Applications

- Business Location Type cross-reference, repeating group consisting of:
  - Business Location Type
  - frequency (per day).

Effect Correspondence Diagram

The Effect Correspondence Diagram is as defined in the *SSADM Version 4 Reference Manual* with the addition of an Access Type (per entity node), where access type is C(reate), M(odify), D(elete) or R(ead).

Event	Walk In Rental
Mode	Critical online
Function	Walk In Rental
Frequency	50 per day
Description	To create a rental for a customer who does not have a reservation
Business location	Frequency
Branch Office	50 per day

Table 5.2: An example of an event definition

5.9.3 Derivation

The derivation of the Event Package product is from:

- Requirements Catalogue
- Function Definition
- Entity Life Histories
- Logical Data Model.

5.9.4 Quality criteria

For the event definition:

1 are all of the components complete?

2 has an Effect Correspondence Diagram been produced?

For the Event Package, does the package provide a complete specification of the update processing required to support a single event?

Chapter 5
Product structure and descriptions

5.9.5 External dependencies — To be reviewed by relevant users.

5.10 Enquiry Package — This product is an aggregation and extension of the enquiry (identified as part of function definition) and Enquiry Access Path (produced using logical data modelling) as defined in the *SSADM Version 4 Reference Manual*. See Table 5.3 for an Enquiry form.

5.10.1 Purpose — To define the enquiries that are required within the system in support of user decisions and functions. This aggregation is a standard requirement of SSADM Version 4 but is extended to provide additional information of importance in client/server developments. Thus, the Enquiry Package is extended to provide a cross-reference to the Business Location Types from which they originate, their mode of operation (for example critical on-line) and their detailed volumetrics (such as daily volume for each Business Location Type).

Note that as enquiries emanate from functions as defined in core SSADM, any mode of operation attached to an enquiry is automatically attached to the function: that is, if the enquiry is critical on-line, so must be the function.

The Enquiry Package will be taken forward into Logical System Specification and Physical Design as the encapsulation of system access and will provide a full logical definition of the elements of system functionality that must be supported by the new client/server system.

5.10.2 Composition — The composition of the Enquiry Package product is:
- enquiry definition
- function name/identifier
- enquiry name/identifier
- description
- mode (for example batch, on-line, critical on-line)
- frequency (per day)

SSADM and Client/Server Applications

- Business Location Type cross–reference, repeating group consisting of:
    - Business Location Type
    - frequency (per day)
- Enquiry Access Path as defined in core SSADM with the possibility of a Read Operations List.

Enquiry	Available Cars
Mode	Online
Associated functions	Book Car, Record Agreement For Transfer, Walk in Rental, Write Off Car
Description	To check the local car database to locate the available resources for a particular group
Frequency	95 per day
Business Location	Frequency
Branch Office	95 per day

Table 5.3: An example of an Enquiry Form.

5.10.3 Derivation

The derivation of the Enquiry Package product is from:

- Requirements Catalogue
- Function Definition
- Logical Data Model.

5.10.4 Quality criteria

For the enquiry definition:

1 are all of the components complete?

2 has an Enquiry Access Path been produced?

For the Enquiry Package, does the package provide a complete specification of the enquiry processing required to support a single enquiry?

5.10.5 External dependencies

To be reviewed by relevant users.

Chapter 5
Product structure and descriptions

5.11 Entity Access Matrix

This product is an extension of the Event/Entity Matrix as defined in the *SSADM Version 4 Reference Manual*. The Event/Entity Matrix is a working product used to assist in the production of Effect Correspondence Diagrams (ECD)s and Entity Life Histories (ELH)s. Its use has been changed in this volume so that it is updated in line with development of ECDs and ELHs and is retained as part of the processing specification.

5.11.1 Purpose

The Entity Access Matrix is an extension of the Event/Entity Matrix. It provides a summary of the way in which events update the Logical Data Model and the way in which enquiries access the Logical Data Model. It is especially useful in the validation of the processing specification as it is easily apparent when for example, entities have not been updated, created or used. For an example, see to Figure 6.2 in Chapter 6.

5.11.2 Composition

The Entity Access Matrix contains the following information:

- all events required to maintain the Logical Data Model in a state concurrent with the external world it models
- all required enquiries
- all entities
- access type. The way in which each event/enquiry updates/accesses the relevant entity. Access type may be C(reate), M(odify), D(elete) for events and R(ead) for events and enquiries.

5.11.3 Derivation

The derivation of the Entity Access Matrix product is from:

- Requirements Catalogue
- Required System Logical Data Model
- Function Definitions.

5.11.4 Quality criteria

The quality criteria are:

1 are all entities from the Logical Data Model listed along one axis of the matrix?

2 are all events/enquiries listed along the other axis of the matrix?

3 is each entity created by at least one event?

4 is each entity modified and deleted by at least one event? If not, why not?

5 is each entity read by at least one event/enquiry? If not, why not?

6 does each event update at least one entity?

7 does each enquiry access at least one entity?

8 has consideration been made for entities that are going to be created by the target system?

5.11.5 External dependencies

None.

5.12 Technical System Architecture

This product is an addition to the SSADM Version 4 product set and forms part of the method's Policies and Procedures model (within the System Development Template).

5.12.1 Purpose

The Technical System Architecture is used to describe the components of the hardware and software infrastructure necessary to support the client/server applications supporting the organisation's business and technical strategies. It specifies:

- the physical architecture
- the standards to be adhered to
- the system software components of the operational environment
- the tool set required for development.

This physical architecture is specified through the definition of its components and a mapping of these components to components of the Conceptual Model and External Design (part of the 3–schema specification architecture).

The purpose of the Technical System Architecture is to provide information about the technical constraints on the applications and the development project, so that the practitioner can ensure that:

Chapter 5
Product structure and descriptions

- the chosen architecture is capable of supporting the organisation's business and technical strategies
- the evolving nature of client/server technology, both operational and developmental, can be catered for (and does not impose unnecessary risks)
- the chosen technical components combine to form a feasible architecture that is able to satisfy the quantified non-functional requirements
- prototyping and piloting of the technical architecture and the application it supports is facilitated.

The objective is to define a stable and robust model of the optimum technical architecture for the application.

5.12.2 Composition

The Technical System Architecture is composed of a set of platforms interconnected by message channels and is supported by a mapping of the client and server partitions:

- Platform Description (see section 5.13)
- Message Channel Description (see section 5.14)
- Standard Mapping (see section 5.15)
- Application Programming Interface standards. A textual description of standards that application designers and programmers must adhere to when designing/constructing application components to execute on the platforms concerned
- special components. A high level textual description of components of the technical architecture that will be required as a result of the adoption of a client/server infrastructure (for example, a notification strategy when an attempt is made by two clients trying to update the same data on the server).

Technical System Architectures that have been excluded should be noted and briefly described. It may be important to understand the basis under which a model was rejected.

SSADM and Client/Server Applications

5.12.3 Derivation
The derivation of the Technical System Architecture product is from:
- Feasibility Report
- Selected Technical System Option
- selected Distribution Option
- Requirements Catalogue
- User Catalogue
- Business Location Types
- Workstation Types.

5.12.4 Quality criteria
The quality criteria are:
1. is the set of Platform Descriptions and Message Channel Definitions complete and consistent?
2. does the set have at least one platform and at least one Message Channel?
3. does the Standard Mapping meet all of the critical technical requirements?
4. does the Standard Mapping encompass all of the components of the conceptual schema and external design?
5. have all relevant standards been documented or referenced?
6. have all special components been described?

5.12.5 External dependencies
Clear management (technical and business) decision.

5.13 Platform Description
This product is an addition to the SSADM Version 4 product set and forms part of the method's Policies and Procedures model (within the System Development Template). It is a component of the new product, Technical System Architecture.

5.13.1 Purpose
A platform is a combination of hardware and software components that interoperate and provide an operational environment (or part thereof) in which application program components can execute. A Platform Description identifies any available platform and defines

Chapter 5
Product structure and descriptions

the services that it will offer the logical/conceptual system.

5.13.2 Composition

The composition of the Platform Description product (see Figure 5.4) is:

- identifier/name
- layer (for example presentation, application or data)
- location (such as client or server)
- textual description

ID	
Layer	Data
Client/Server	Server
Description	Oracle RDBMS running on ICL DRS series mini computer
Component*	Oracle RDBMS
Cornerstone component	Yes
Reason for selection	Company standard
Availability	6am – 9pm
Procurement cost	
Skills required	Database manager
Training costs	£3,000
Standards	
Dependency on other components	UNIX operating system ICL DRS computer
Application software	Accounts update (PR0045) Stock inventory (PR0043)
Workstation types	
* Component and subsequent fields are a repeating group	

Figure 5.4: An example of a Platform Description

- a set of Platform Components consisting of:
    - name/identifier
    - textual description
    - indicator denoting whether the component is a cornerstone component of the platform (that is, it dictates which other components can be used)
    - reason for selection
    - availability (such as server available between 8am and 6pm)
    - procurement cost
    - skills requirement
    - training costs
    - relevant standard (for example UNIX)
    - dependency on/compatibility with other platform components (repeating group)
    - a required set of application software components to be generated by this application development project, each with a clearly defined interface
    - Workstation Types supported by platforms of this kind – this set may be null if no workstations are directly supported (repeating group).

Platforms and platform components that have been excluded should be noted and briefly described. It may be important to understand the basis under which a platform/component was rejected.

5.13.3 Derivation

The derivation of the Platform Description product is from:

- Requirements Catalogue
- User Catalogue
- outline required environment description
- Business System Options.

5.13.4 Quality criteria

The quality criteria are:

1 is the platform fully described?

2 have all relevant components of each platform been identified and defined?

3 are the relationships between platforms and platform components consistent?

Chapter 5
Product structure and descriptions

    4 is the platform dedicated to the application and if not, have all the capacity issues been catered for?

    5 has every applicable cornerstone (that is, any platform component that derives other platform components) been identified?

5.13.5 External dependencies

Technical information from platform component suppliers.

5.14 Message Channel Description

This product is an addition to the SSADM Version 4 product set and forms part of the method's Policies and Procedures model (within the System Development Template). It is a component of the new product, Technical System Architecture.

5.14.1 Purpose

A message channel is a connection between two platforms that is capable of transferring messages, for example a Local Area Network, a modem connection, or a Datex_P connection. Message channels exhibit particular characteristics for the transmission of message traffic, such as the transmission rate or transmission cost. They impose constraints on applications conforming to the Technical System Architecture.

5.14.2 Composition

The composition of the Message Channel Description product is:

- name/identifier
- textual description
- platforms connected (repeating group)
- minimum, maximum and mean transmission rate
- response times
- transmission cost
- error correction provisions/strategy
- details of any dependencies on outside agencies (for instance, PSDN).

Message channels that have been excluded should be noted and briefly described. It may be important to understand the basis under which a message channel was rejected.

SSADM and Client/Server Applications

5.14.3 Derivation

The derivation of the Message Channel Description product is from:

- Requirements Catalogue
- User Catalogue
- outline required environment description
- Business System Options.

5.14.4 Quality criteria

The quality criteria are:

1 Is the message channel fully described?

2 Are the cross-references to Platform Descriptions consistent?

5.14.5 External dependencies

Technical information from external suppliers.

5.15 Standard Mapping

This product is an addition to the SSADM Version 4 product set. It is a component of the new product, Technical System Architecture and part of Client/Server Design.

5.15.1 Purpose

The Standard Mapping defines on which platform each element of the system's conceptual schema (that is, Logical Data Model, events and enquiries) and user interface will be supported. This is an ideal mapping which may prove not to lead to an effective implementation. It provides the default Client/Server Design based on information available in advance of detailed design, evaluation and tuning.

5.15.2 Composition

As each specification element may map to a different platform component, the Standard Mapping is a repeating group of:

- specification element (such as the Logical Data Model, entity, Event Package, Enquiry Package, dialogue/window)
- platform.

This is best defined using a simple mapping diagram (see Figure 5.5).

Chapter 5
Product structure and descriptions

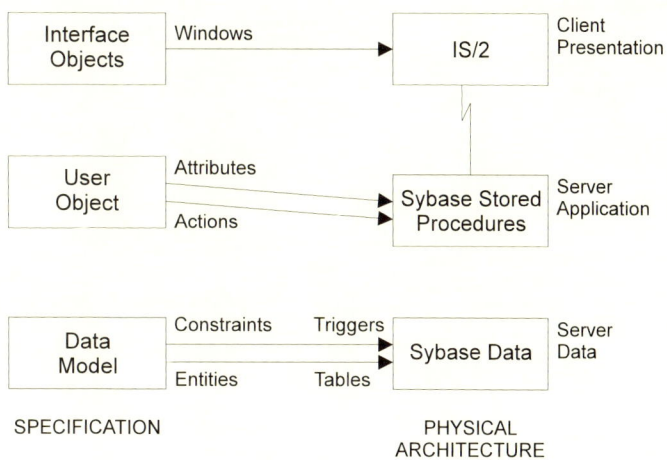

Figure 5.5: Standard Mapping

5.15.3 Derivation

The derivation of the Standard Mapping product is from:

- Logical Data Model
- Event Package
- Enquiry Package
- user interface design (dialogue/window)
- Platform Description.

5.15.4 Quality criteria

The quality criteria are:

1 have all of the conceptual schema and interface design components been included?

2 have all of the platforms been included?

3 are the mappings consistent (for example, one platform per specification component)?

5.15.5 External dependencies

None.

5.16 Client/Server Design

This product is an addition to the SSADM Version 4 product set and forms part of the method's Internal Design (within the System Development Template).

SSADM and Client/Server Applications

5.16.1 Purpose

The Client/Server Design provides a precise specification of which platform components (such as the C programming language and dynamic linked libraries) will host the various instances of Conceptual Model component (for instance, the Event Package) and the interfacing components (see Figure 5.1). In effect it is a detailed mapping and consequently is based on the Standard Mapping produced as part of the Technical System Architecture (see Figure 5.5). The Client/Server Design will differ from the Standard Mapping, in most cases, since the non-functional requirements of the system will force a deviation from the simple design approach adopted during technical architecture definition. Potentially conflicting issues such as integrity and speed are likely to make system implementation according to Standard Mapping technically infeasible.

5.16.2 Composition

The composition of the Client/Server Design product is a repeating group of:

- specification instance (for example, a Customer entity)
- platform component (such as an Oracle table)
- repeating group consisting of, where the detailed mapping differs from the Standard Mapping:
  - non-functional requirement
  - mapping explanation.

It also includes a repeating group of special components (for instance, a notification scheme), consisting of:

- name/identifier
- textual description
- cross-reference to specification instance (such as an Event Package implementing notification scheme), repeating group.

5.16.3 Derivation

The derivation of the Client/Server Design product is from:

- Logical Data Model
- Event Package
- Enquiry Package

Chapter 5
Product structure and descriptions

- user interface design (dialogue/window)
- Technical System Architecture.

5.16.4 Quality criteria

The quality criteria are:

1 have all instances of all conceptual schema/user interface components been included?

2 have all of the platforms been included?

3 are the mappings consistent (for example, one platform per specification component)?

4 does the design meet all critical technical requirements?

5 does the design satisfy the remaining non-functional requirements?

5.16.5 External dependencies

Users to agree any changes in requirements necessary to produce an effective design.

Users and operations representatives to join review team.

Users to agree any operations/management rules to which procedures will be subject.

5.17 Task Model

This product is an addition to the SSADM Version 4 product set and forms part of the method's User Environment (within the System Development Template). It is used to help derive the User Catalogue.

5.17.1 Purpose

The Task Model defines the job activity descriptions of the users and details the tasks that are performed relevant to the target system(s).

5.17.2 Composition

The composition of the Task Model product is a repeating group of:

- task or job activity description
- business location where task is performed
- task/Data Flow Model process cross–reference.

5.17.3 Derivation

The derivation of the Task Model product is from:

- Business Location Type
- Data Flow Model.

SSADM and Client/Server Applications

5.17.4 Quality criteria

The quality criteria are:

1 have all tasks relevant to use of the target system(s) been identified?

2 have all Data Flow Model processes been assigned a task?

3 can all tasks identified be associated with a Business Location Type?

5.17.5 External dependencies

None.

Chapter 6
Techniques

6 Techniques

6.1 Introduction

Chapter 4 identified the changes to product structure and descriptions required to core SSADM in order to support the development of client/server applications. This chapter will detail all of the techniques that must be extended or added in order to use SSADM for the development of client/server systems.

This chapter is introduced via the System Development Template (SDT), which shows the techniques that are used in the SSADM and client/server method. Most of the technique descriptions are detailed to the same extent as in the *SSADM Version 4 Reference Manual*. A few techniques, however, will be presented via a brief description and the reader will be referred to other volumes within the ISE Library for further details.

6.2 Summary of technique changes

This section lists the new, altered and extended techniques.

The new techniques are:

- business area modelling (see section 6.5)
- client design (see section 6.9)
- client/server partitioning (see section 6.8)
- server design (see section 6.10)
- technical architecture definition (see section 6.7).

The altered or extended techniques are:

- entity-event modelling (see section 6.6)
- physical process specification extended by client design and server design (see section 6.8)
- requirements definition (see section 6.4)
- technical system options (see section 6.11).

There are no replaced techniques.

SSADM and Client/Server Applications

6.3 SSADM, client/server and the SDT from a technique point of view

Figure 6.1 shows the SDT and embedded 3–schema specification architecture (3–SSA) structure of the major techniques required for SSADM and client/server.

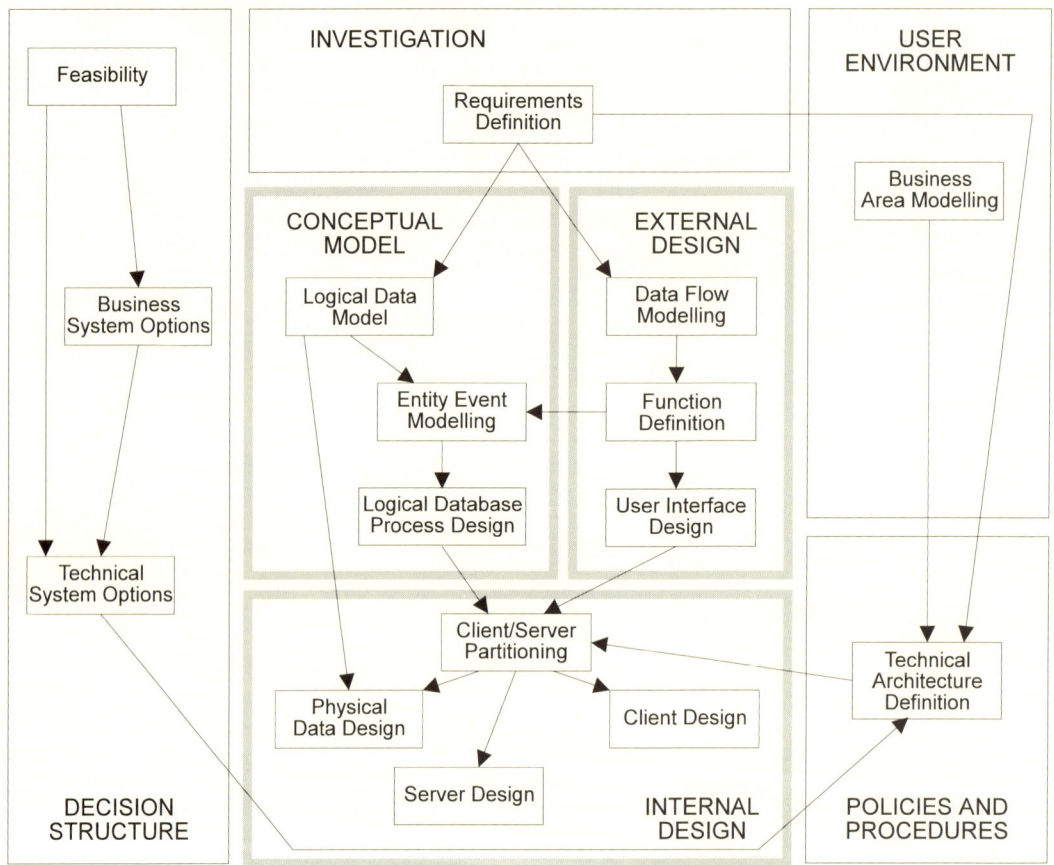

Figure 6.1: SDT and Embedded 3–SSA from a Technique Point of View

6.4 Requirements definition

Requirements definition for client/server applications proceeds as is usual for core SSADM projects. However, greater emphasis is placed on the quantification of non–functional requirements (NFRs) and the early identification of critical technical requirements, a subset of NFRs.

6.4.1 Purpose

The fulfilment of non-functional requirements is critical to the success of an application. Non-functional criteria

Chapter 6
Techniques

need to be set during the initial analysis stage of a development. They can then be used to assess the quality of the application in terms of:

- how suitable the application is for providing IT support to the business activities carried out by users. Does it provide the correct set of functions to the right sets of users?

- does the application provide the required inter-operation with other applications executing in the same technical environment?

- is it secure? Does the application protect itself from unauthorized and/or accidental access?

- is the application reliable? Is it available when needed, tolerant of faults, recoverable and testable?

- can defects in the application be corrected quickly and at an acceptable cost?

- is the integrity of the data retained in the application assured?

- how easy/expensive is it to add additional Enquiry Types not recognized during the initial development?

- how easy/expensive is it to adapt the application to cater for changes in the competitive and legislative business environment?

- is the software sufficiently portable? Does it conform to the prescribed standards? Does it deliver reusable components? Can individual components be replaced with limited effect on other components? Can it be installed easily/cheaply at the correct set of Business Locations?

- how well does the application support user interaction? Does it minimise operator effort and user error rates? Does it maximise learnability, productivity and memorability?

- does it perform sufficiently well with respect to the consumption of computer resources (such as RAM or CPU cycles) and the consumption of material, energy and funds?

SSADM and Client/Server Applications

Client/Server Design   The justification for the adoption of client/server technology is related to non-functional requirements. Therefore early in a project we need to expose what is required from the client/server application. This may be:

- is the functionality suitable, and do the distributed functions provide the required utility (for example, continuity of service, local ownership of data or the support for correct number of users)?

- are the development costs minimised?

- is the design stable (for instance, has it the ability to add business locations without degrading response time and throughput rates)?

- is it robust – what must each Business Location Type be able to do in the event of a communications failure? How soon must normal service be resumed?

- does it provide consistency – what parts of the application are allowed to be loosely co-ordinated (that is they may be temporarily inconsistent)? Within what timescales must they be made consistent?

- what are the constraints on distribution, such as architectural standards, compatibility with already installed technology, procurement policies, existing geographic sites, requirements for inter-operation with other applications?

Applications are developed to meet business needs and provide business benefits. One way such benefits can be undermined by an otherwise functionally complete application is by failing to meet the non-functional quality expectations imposed by users.

6.4.2 Where used   As in core SSADM, Requirements Definition is an iterative technique where the Requirements Catalogue may be referenced, checked and updated at any time.

6.4.3 Relationship to other techniques   Requirements definition in SSADM and client/server retains the same relationships to other techniques as in core SSADM. It is also related to:

- business area modelling – which provides an analysis of the business environment and is likely to be the source of the majority of NFRs

- technical architecture definition – which will use the NFRs in the specification and evaluation of a technical architecture

- client/server partitioning – which will use the NFRs to determine the required Client/Server Design

- client design – which will use the NFRs in the specification and evaluation of client functionality. (Functional requirements will have been taken into account in the specification of Events and Enquiries)

- server design – which will use the NFRs in the specification and evaluation of server functionality. (Functional requirements will have been taken into account in the specification of events and enquiries).

6.4.4 Concepts and notation

The functional requirements remain defined as in core SSADM. The non-functional requirements (NFR) are expanded to give more details than that required in the core method.

Critical technical requirements

The critical technical requirements are a subset of NFRs. They place major demands and constraints on the technical architecture of the system and thus the Client/Server Design. They are, in effect, mandatory NFRs.

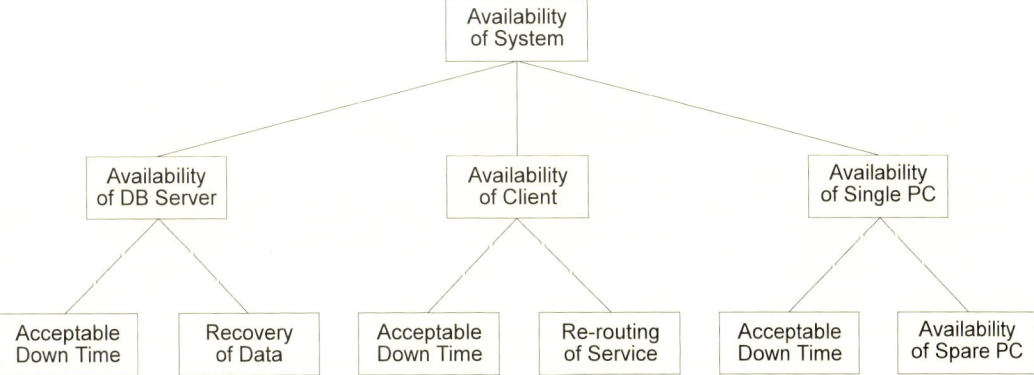

Figure 6.2: NFR Structure

Where the technical architecture of the application has been determined outside the project, the critical technical requirements will be used to assess the feasibility of the project and the feasibility of a client/server solution. Where the technical architecture is to be determined within the scope of the project, the critical technical requirements provide a set of mandatory requirements against which Technical System Options can be evaluated and selected.

The NFR Structure in Figure 6.2 is a type of SSADM structure diagram where nodes represent NFRs. Each node of the structure can be decomposed into two or more subnodes which represent component requirements. Branch nodes, especially towards the top of the structure, can be expressed in general or business terms. Leaf nodes must be expressed in quantifiable terms.

6.4.5 Procedure

The procedure for requirements definition is the same as in core SSADM in the area of identifying and describing requirements. There are however, three additional steps that should be overlaid for the definition of NFRs.

Structure NFRs

The NFRs that have been identified should be organised into an NFR Structure. The objective is to produce a hierarchy of NFRs which are expressed in business/general terms at its top and can be expressed in precise, measurable terms at its leaf nodes.

Quantify NFRs

Requirements located at leaf nodes of the NFR Structure should be fully defined in terms of a scale of measure, test of achieved level, current/target level, high and low tolerance levels, cost of not attaining target level and benefit of attaining target level.

Identify critical technical requirements

The NFR Structure should be reviewed and those requirements that place mandatory demands or constraints on the technical architecture should be identified.

6.5 Business area modelling

Business area modelling seeks to provide a model of the business environment the proposed application is going to work in. It will assist in identifying requirements and

Chapter 6
Techniques

in fully representing the classes and characteristics of users.

Business area modelling is not a mandatory technique within SSADM and client/server and hence will not be fully described in this section.

6.5.1 Purpose

The purpose of business area modelling is to understand the relevant characteristics of the various populations of application users and the tasks performed by these users. This understanding will provide a source for requirements, Business Location Types and Workstation Types.

A description of user classes is required to direct the process of client design to ensure that it can handle the range of user skills and capabilities identified.

A description of user tasks/processes is required to ensure that system functionality is specified and located such that it will support business activities.

6.5.2 Where used

Business area modelling can be used during Feasibility and Requirements Analysis to assist in gaining a thorough understanding of the application's business environment.

6.5.3 Relationship to other techniques

Requirements definition – information gathered during Business Area Analysis will be used as a source of requirements.

Technical architecture definition – Business Location Types and Workstation Types will be identified from the products of business area modelling.

6.5.4 Reference

A detailed definition of business area modelling can be found in the User Analysis and Task Modelling sections of the ISE library volume *SSADM and GUI Design: a Project Manager's Guide*.

6.6 Entity-event modelling

Entity-event modelling for client/server applications remains largely unchanged from the core definition. However, to provide an appropriate level of detail on the definition of system functionality, there has been some consolidation and enhancement.

77

SSADM and Client/Server Applications

The Event/Entity Matrix is extended to include enquiries and is renamed the Entity Access Matrix. Events and enquiries are all defined on this matrix and modelled using Effect Correspondence Diagrams and Enquiry Access Paths. Events and enquiries are also extended to provide additional information required for the design of client/server systems.

The production of Entity Life Histories remains unchanged.

This section only details the elements of entity-event modelling that have been changed in SSADM and client/server. All other aspects are as defined in core SSADM.

6.6.1 Purpose

The purpose of entity-event modelling is to provide a logical specification of the required system processing. The addition of business location information allows the system design to take account of the required location for system processing. Thus, certain processing will be required at certain places as will certain subsets of data.

In essence, the products of this technique will encapsulate the application's business logic.

6.6.2 Where used

Entity-event modelling is used during Requirements Specification to produce a definition of the application's required processing.

6.6.3 Relationship to other techniques

Entity-event modelling in SSADM and client/server retains the same relationships to other techniques as in core SSADM. However, certain relationships, especially the new ones, are particularly important in SSADM and client/server. Entity-event modelling relates to:

- logical data modelling – the Logical Data Model contains entities and attributes that will be accessed and updated by events and enquiries. The LDM will be analysed in order to identify the events required to maintain the data in a correct state. Finally, the definition of events and enquiries will be validated against the Logical Data Model, both directly and through the production of Entity Life Histories

Chapter 6
Techniques

- technical architecture definition – will use cross-reference information concerning events/enquiries, Business Location Types and volumetrics in order to determine the Standard Mapping and the required Platform and Message components

- client/server partitioning – will map instances of events and enquiries on to elements of the Technical System Architecture

- client design – will produce designs for the implementation of events and enquiries on client-based Technical System Architecture components

- server design – will produce designs for the implementation of events and enquiries on server-based Technical System Architecture components.

6.6.4 Concepts and notation

Event identification from the Logical Data Model

Core SSADM describes a method of identifying events which is performed during function definition. Under this method, events (predominantly business events) are identified from flows across the boundary of the Data Flow Model and form part of the definition of the relevant function.

SSADM and client/server propose the derivation of the requirements for changes from analysis of the Logical Data Model. These changes can be caused by one or more events. It is important to identify those events that are required to maintain the integrity of the system data. These events are often system triggered (for example, a stock level has fallen below an acceptable level) or time triggered (such as at 12 midnight all remote records should have their currency flag reset). Such events may or may not be directly linked to the business events that will have been identified during function definition. The identification of such events may place constraints on the partitioning of system data and functionality or may identify the need for additional architecture components.

Once these events have been identified, it is important to reconcile them with the business events defined during function definition.

79

Event location · For client/server applications, it is important to identify the locations where particular events and enquiries will be initiated and where in the function definition these occur. If, for example, an enquiry is only initiated at a single Business Location Type, it may be desirable to locate the relevant data within this Business Location Type. For example, the case for such a decision would be strengthened if volumetrics for the enquiry far outweighed those for the event/s updating the data if these were not to be located within the same Business Location Type. In the same way, volumetrics information must also be a consideration in the event of multiple locations.

6.6.5 Procedure · This section defines the changed procedure within entity-event modelling as regards the production of Enquiry and Event Packages. The procedure related to Entity Life Histories remains as defined in core SSADM.

Identify and document events · Events identified during function definition should be added to the Entity Access Matrix.

The Logical Data Model should be analysed to identify additional events. Examine every entity in the LDM for events in the following categories:

- birth – each entity must have its own distinct birth event unless:
    - it is a detail entity of a master entity which is invalid without any details (the birth of the master is also that of the detail)
    - it is a master entity which is born at the same time as its first detail entity
    - it is an entity created, updated and deleted by another application and used in this application only for reference (read-only) purposes

- death – there are two kinds of death event, the 'update death' (after which the entity may not be updated) and the 'history death' (after which it may be deleted). For some entities the same event fulfils both purposes. An entity will have its own distinct update death, unless:
    - its death immediately follows its birth
    - it shares the death event of one of its masters

- state change – such events usually 'freeze' or 'thaw' the entity in some way. To 'freeze' an entity is to move it into a state where some types of event are no longer permitted to affect it. To 'thaw' it is to move it into a state where the events are again permitted

- date/time – such events record the passing of time or of a particular business milestone (such as a month-end)

- master relationship change (Table 6.1) – such events cause an entity's relationship with each of its masters to be tied, cut or swapped. They will be dependent on the type of relationship

Relationship Type	Operation	Trigger Event
fixed/mandatory	tie	birth of this entity
fixed/optional	tie	possible birth, may be 'delayed notification'
changeable/mandatory	tie	birth of this entity
changeable/mandatory	*swap	specific swap event
changeable/mandatory	*swap	death of master (detail switched to alternative master)
changeable/optional	tie	possible birth of this entity
changeable/optional	cut	possible death of this entity
changeable/optional	cut	possible specific cut event
changeable/optional	*swap	possible specific swap event

* Where 'swap' events are identified, the master event should be annotated since two instances of the master are involved (for example, a transfer between two accounts). In a distributed application the two instances may be stored at different locations.

Table 6.1: Master Relationship Change

- detail relationship change (Table 6.2) – identify events that cause masters to gain or lose a detail. They are the events that cause details to be cut, tied or swapped

Relationship Type	Operation	Trigger Event
fixed (mandatory from the detail's viewpoint)	gain	mandatory birth of the detail entity
fixed (optional from the detail's viewpoint)	gain	possible birth event of the detail entity, may be 'delayed master notification'
changeable	gain	optional tie or swap event of the detail entity
changeable	lose	optional cut or swap event of the detail entity

Table 6.2: Detail Relationship Change

- non-key attribute change (Table 6.3) – identify the events that cause entity attributes (other than primary and foreign key attributes) to be updated

Relationship Type	Operation	Trigger Event
fixed attributes	store	birth of this entity
fixed attributed	store	possible 'late notification' event?
changeable attribute	store	probable birth of this entity
changeable attribute	change value	probable simple, distinct update event
optional attribute	set null	possible birth of this entity
optional attribute	set null	possible event that removes this entity from the criteria for selection on this attribute

Table 6.3: Non-key Attribute Change

Chapter 6
Techniques

Identify enquiries   Enquiries identified from the Requirements Catalogue (during function definition) should be added to the Entity Access Matrix.

Produce the Entity   Once all events and enquiries have been added to the
Access Matrix   matrix the definition of the matrix should be completed. Hence, each event/enquiry should reside in its own row of the matrix as shown below in Figure 6.2. Where the event/enquiry requires access to the an entity, the Access Type, that is, C(reate), M(odify), D(elete) and/or R(ead) should be placed in the appropriate cell.

Entity/Event	Customer	Account	Warehouse	Sales Office	Order	Order Line	Invoice	Stock
New	R/C	R/C			C	C		
Customer	R	R			R	R	R	
Invoice		R				R	R	
Stock			R					R
Delete	R	R			D	D		
Modify	R	R			M	C/D		

Figure 6.2: An example Entity Access Matrix

Fully Define Events   Following the completion of the Entity Access Matrix,
and Enquiries   the Event and Enquiry Packages should be started. For each event/enquiry:

- the mode should be determined as batch, on-line, critical on-line or other with reference to the defined non-functional Requirements. This information will be used during client/server partitioning, and beyond, to determine the most appropriate platform for the element of processing

- the frequency should be determined (generally per day). This information is also used to determine the most appropriate platform for an element of processing and is especially useful where compromises have to be made (for example, should the event be placed on a head-office server where it

83

SSADM and Client/Server Applications

will be executed many times a day or on a satellite server where it will provide the user with the best response time). This total figure should be the sum of frequencies for each Business Location Type which will originate them

- a list of Business Location Types from which the element of processing may originate should be compiled. Each will be expressed together with a frequency. Where the mode of the element differs at different Business Location Types, it may be expressed at the Business Location Type level rather than at the event/enquiry level.

Reconcile events with Data Flow Model	The application will recognize time based events (for example, change of date) and milestone events (such as the start of financial year). All other events should be recognizable as inputs from external entities on the Required Data Flow Model. All DFM inputs should be represented as events. Inconsistencies should be rectified.
Analyse the Entity Access Matrix	Appropriate organisation of the Entity Access Matrix may be required to facilitate certain analysis, eg by Business Location Type, Mode or Access Type. Hence, it is desirable to document the matrix on a medium that allows easy manipulation (eg a CASE tool).
Complete Event and Enquiry Packages	The Event and Enquiries Packages should be completed with the production of Effect Correspondence Diagrams and Enquiry Access Paths. These conform to the normal approach adopted in core SSADM except that ECD entity nodes are annotated with the appropriate access type from the Entity Access Matrix. ECDs and EAPs may have operations lists.
6.7 **Technical architecture definition**	Technical architecture definition seeks to describe the components of the hardware and software infrastructure necessary to support the client/server applications supporting the organisation's business and technical strategies.
	It is used to specify the physical architecture, the standards to be adhered to, the system software components of the operational environment and the tool set required for development.

Chapter 6
Techniques

6.7.1 Purpose

The purpose of technical architecture definition is to provide information about the technical constraints on the application and the development project, so that the SSADM practitioner can ensure that:

- the chosen architecture is capable of supporting the organisation's business and technical strategies
- the evolving nature of client/server technology, both operational and developmental, can be catered for (and does not impose unnecessary risks)
- the chosen technical components combine to form a feasible architecture that is able to satisfy the critical technical requirements and, at a lower level of granularity, the quantified non-functional requirements
- prototyping and piloting of the technical architecture and the application it supports are facilitated.

The objective is to define a stable and robust model of the optimum technical architecture for the application.

6.7.2 Where used

Technical architecture definition is used as part of technical system options to define in detail the Selected Technical System Option and the Technical System Architecture replaces the Technical Environment Description product in this Stage.

6.7.3 Relationship to other techniques

The techniques that have a relationship with technical architecture definition are:

- business area modelling – where Business Location Types and Workstation Types are identified
- requirements definition – where the non-functional requirements are recorded
- technical system options – where the selected TSO will be further defined by the Technical System Architecture
- client/server partitioning – where the Event and Enquiry Packages developed in entity-event modelling are mapped onto the Technical System Architecture to create the Standard Mapping and provide the basis for Client/Server Design. Figure

SSADM and Client/Server Applications

6.4 illustrates an example of how events and enquiries can be mapped onto each Platform Component within the Technical Architecture Component.

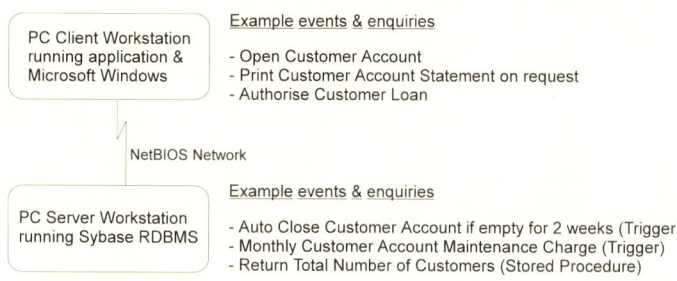

Figure. 6.4: Example of Event/Enquiry to Platform Component Mapping

6.7.4 Concepts and notation	As a replacement for the Technical Environment Description, the Technical System Architecture must address all areas covered by the Technical Environment Description in core SSADM as well as the additional client/server descriptions.
	Notification Strategies are best introduced here as they are made use of by this technique. Figure 6.5 show the two main notification strategies.
Strategy 1	Each interface object notifies other interface objects when a significant update occurs. The other interface objects may either use the notification data to update themselves, or refresh their view from the database. A possible mechanism is to broadcast a message with the type and identity of the object that has been updated. Note that responsibility for notifying and for updating (upon receipt of notification) lies with the user interface objects.
Strategy 2	When an entity is updated it notifies all user interface objects which are viewing it that it has been updated, so that the user interface objects know to refresh their windows.

Chapter 6
Techniques

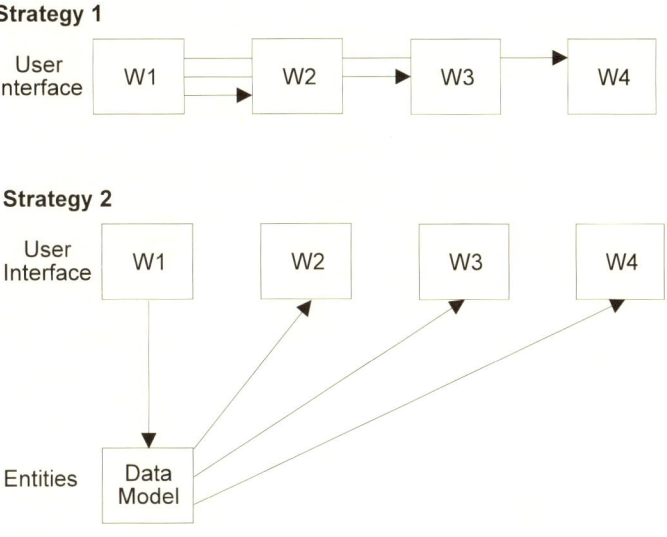

Figure 6.5: Notification strategies

These strategies may be mixed. It is also possible to have fine-grain exceptions. For example most updating on a user interface object may use one strategy, but a particular user action may use a different mechanism.

The Platform Descriptions and Message Channel Descriptions are textual documents as set out in the product descriptions in Chapter 5.

6.7.5 Procedure

Technical architectures are described as a set of Platforms, each consisting of a collection of inter-operating software and hardware, connected by a set of Message Channels that provide and constrain the means of communication between platforms.

The first step is to select the number of topographical levels the Technical System Architecture is required to have.

This choice is made with reference to the non-functional requirements for the fault tolerance, robustness and consistency of the application. For instance, a list of factors to be taken into account may include the following:

SSADM and Client/Server Applications

- do semi-autonomous Business Location Types require to continue processing in the case of a communications failure?

- how inconsistent (out of date with the external world and with each other) are Business Locations permitted to get?

- what are the constraints on recovery of a complete, self-consistent application?

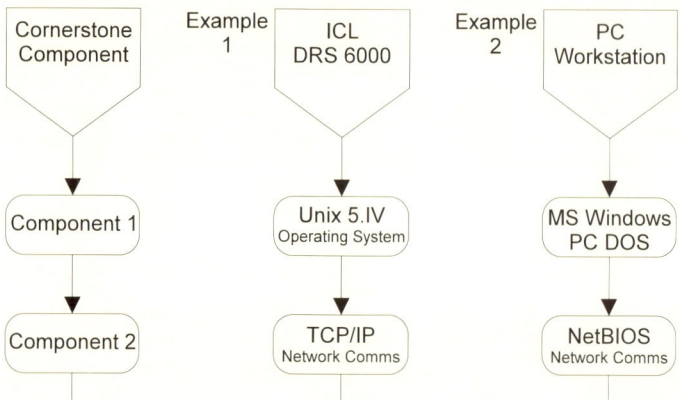

Figure 6.5: *Examples of cornerstone components*

The answers to these and similar questions dictate the capabilities (for instance, the processing power or local data storage) desired of the platforms chosen.

The next step is to define a cornerstone component for each platform. This is a hardware or software component that will determine the selection of other, compatible, components (see Figure 6.5). The cornerstone component thus provides a stable baseline for the selection of the remainder of the Technical System Architecture. Choice of such a cornerstone component is often constrained by the need for compatibility with and/or migration from existing applications and stored data. For example, in Figure 6.5, the choice of ICL DRS 6000 Server platform as cornerstone will force the choice of a UNIX operating system and TCP/IP network communications protocol.

Chapter 6
Techniques

The topographical levels and the cornerstone Components dictate the selection of a set of compatible components. These are required to complete the Technical System Architecture. For each cornerstone component, evaluate other components recommended by the suppliers of the cornerstone. If the cornerstone does not provide the required compatible component, or if the performance is inadequate, identify a set of candidate cornerstone and its compatible components and evaluate them against the critical technical requirements.

Compatible components can include hardware, system software, communications software and services and standard (reusable) application components.

The next step is to map the Business Location Types and the Workstation Types onto the components of the topographical layers of the Technical System Architecture. Rules and guidelines for the mapping of logical design components to the physical processors and their systems software are defined and later used in client/server partitioning to define the Standard Mapping.

The technical issues surrounding the concepts of concurrency control and notification are resolved in this technique, specifying how clients are to be kept up to date with information stored centrally and updated by other clients.

Risk analysis is undertaken to ensure that the defined Technical System Architecture will meet the critical technical requirements (and thus is likely to fulfil the more finely grained non-functional requirements).

6.8 Client/Server partitioning

A Client/Server Design must partition the data and functionality in the specification between the layers in the target architecture, and specifically between the client and the server.

6.8.1 Purpose

The purpose of client/server partitioning is to map the logical processing to the components of the Technical System Architecture.

SSADM and Client/Server Applications

6.8.2 Where used — The Standard Mapping created by client/server partitioning forms part of the technical architecture definition and forms part of the further definition of the chosen Technical System Option. However the Standard Mapping is likely to be revised during physical data design as the data distribution is optimized.

6.8.3 Relationship to other techniques — Client/Server partitioning is closely related to technical architecture definition and forms part of the Technical System Architecture.

The Event and Enquiry Packages defined in entity-event modelling are mapped onto the Technical System Architecture.

6.8.4 Concepts and notation — The set of Standard Mappings is made up of a collection of standard SSADM products.

6.8.5 Procedure — The client/server partitioning technique addresses partitioning in a systematic way, considering in turn how each layer of the specification will be implemented. The data model is mapped into physical components first, followed by the application processes (events, enquiries), and finally the user interface. This allows each layer to be designed to exploit components and facilities in the previous layers.

Achieving the best partitioning frequently requires some iteration. An initial design provides a basis for workload and performance estimation, which may lead to revisions in the design. Similarly, integration testing of early versions of client and server components may lead to a revised partitioning with a better performance.

6.9 Client design

Client design sets out the detailed physical design and development of the client software components. The events and enquiries identified as client processes in client/server partitioning are developed into Physical Process Specifications.

6.9.1 Purpose — The purpose is to provide a precise specification of the data and functionality at the client level.

6.9.2 Where used — An extension to Physical Process Specification.

6.9.3	Relationship to other techniques	Techniques that have a relationship with client design are:

- client/server partitioning – identifies which Event and Enquiry Packages are to be implemented on the client(s)
- user interface design – defines the standards for the development of the user interface parts of the client design.

6.9.4	Concepts and notation	Client/Server Design is an extension of the Standard Mapping developed in client/server partitioning.
6.9.5	Procedure	The overall structure of client processing is largely determined by the structure of the user interface, in that the program structure corresponds closely to the screen structure.

Inside these programs the logic is typically event-driven. For each event the client program must provide some processing.

Step 1: Predict client performance

Examine the client components identified during client/server partitioning.

For each critical technical requirement identified in the set of non-functional requirements, predict whether client performance is likely to be acceptable.

Performance problems are most likely where:

- there is extensive interaction between screens (or if GUI, then windows)
- there is frequent database access
- very large volumes of data are manipulated.

Where performance will be unacceptable, consider:

- alternative client/server partitionings (for example, some of the more common processing might best be transferred to the server)
- optimising the client design to improve performance.

Step 2: Design client update procedures	Update procedures will have been identified from the Event Packages and mapped onto the Technical System Architecture during client/server partitioning.

Update procedures frequently contain transaction control code, obtaining and releasing write locks or checking time stamps.

If notification strategy 2 (that is, notification at the entity level) is being used, they also send notification messages to other client components informing them that objects have been updated. Specifically, they send messages to components which implement a user interface object containing a view of this user object.

The routing of these notifications may be hard-coded, or may use a subscription mechanism. |
| Step 3: Design Client Enquiry Procedures | Enquiry procedures will have been identified from the Enquiry Packages and mapped onto the Technical System Architecture during client/server partitioning.

Enquiry procedures often include subscription mechanisms to ensure that an interest is registered in an object, so that any changes are notified.

If it is important that the view is stable or consistent, the procedure may obtain a read lock. |
| Step 4: Optimize client for performance | The Client Design should be optimized as in Step 640 (Optimize Physical Data Design) of core SSADM. Particular attention should be paid to the processes that may benefit from being transferred to the server

Strong candidates for converting into server procedures are processes that have:

- high data transfer volumes, there is an opportunity for the data to be pre-processed, filtered, aggregated or condensed on the server
- multiple commands close together, several commands can be chained together on the server. |//
| 6.10 Server design | Server design sets out the detailed design and development of the server software components. The |

Chapter 6
Techniques

events and enquiries identified as server processes in client/server partitioning are developed into Physical Process Specifications.

6.10.1 Purpose	The purpose is to provide a precise specification of the data and functionality at the server level.
6.10.2 Where used	As an extension to Physical Process Specification and Physical Data Design.
6.10.3 Relationship to other techniques	Client/Server partitioning – identifies which Event and Enquiry Packages are to be implemented on the server.
6.10.4 Concepts and notation	Client/Server design is an extension of the Standard Mapping developed in client/server partitioning.
6.10.5 Procedure	This technique includes the design of:

- data-oriented components, such as integrity procedures and triggers
- server application components, such as DBMS stored procedures. TP modules and server processes invoked through remote procedure calls.

Step 1: Design integrity constraints	For each integrity constraint which will be enforced on the server, design how it will be implemented. The three main options are:

- as declarative integrity constraints (for example, a foreign key clause)
- as a trigger (see Step 2)
- as a stored procedure.

A stored procedure may either:

- check whether an update is valid and inform the calling client if there is an error
- maintain the integrity constraint by performing consequential processing.

Types of Integrity Constraints

The types of integrity constraints are:

- referential integrity, this includes:
  - cascade delete to dependent data
  - restrict delete if dependent data exists

93

- nullify the foreign key in the dependent if delete
- cascade key updates to foreign keys in dependents
- restrict key update if dependent data exists
- nullify the foreign keys in the dependent if update.

- relationship cardinality

- relationship exclusivity

- entity cardinality. This will enforce the mandatory maximum or minimum number of entity instances by preventing insertion/deletion.

- derived data. If any derived data is redundantly stored it should be checked that the derived data is updated whenever the base data is modified (for example, each Order may have a value, the sum of which is equal to the Total Order Value attribute of a Customer)

- validity of column values. Validation is to ensure that column values are valid. A range of acceptable values, sometimes referred to as domain constraints, can be applied.

- inter-column constraints

- other integrity rules. Any business rule that can be expressed as a static constraint (or invariant) on the data can be regarded as a data integrity constraint, and can be enforced by server procedures.

Step 2: Design triggers

Several server DBMSs support the concept of a database trigger. A trigger consists of a definition of an event or condition, and a definition of the action to take if the event happens (or the condition becomes true). The action is often in the form of instructions written in a stored procedure language, including calls to other procedures.

As triggers are activated automatically by the DBMS, they are very suitable for enforcing constraints and implementing consequential actions that must always occur.

Chapter 6
Techniques

The main uses of triggers in server design are:

- enforcing referential integrity and other non-application-specific constraints

- maintaining the integrity of redundant and derived data in the database. (Redundant data is stored to improve performance.)

When to use a trigger

Triggers are invisible to the client application, and are compulsory in the sense that a client cannot request to override the triggered processing. For these reasons, triggers are excellent for enforcing compulsory integrity constraints of various kinds.

Triggers are not suitable for processing which is application-specific, or which is optional.

If one application requires some additional processing every time it inserts an entity, but another application requires different processing (or no processing) when it inserts the same entity, a trigger is inappropriate. As events and enquiries are often application-specific, event and enquiry actions and transactions arising from them tend to be application-specific, and not suitable for embedding in triggers.

Similarly, some processing is optional, depending on business rules as to whether or not it is to be applied. For example the calculation of discount on an order may require various calculation routines, or there may be no discount at all. Triggers are inappropriate for optional processing because the business logic outside the triggered routine needs to select the processing to invoke.

However, both application-specific and optional processing can be implemented in stored procedures that are called directly (that is, not triggered.)

Trigger hierarchies

Some databases permit the effect of one trigger to activate another trigger, producing the effect of a

SSADM and Client/Server Applications

hierarchy (or tree) of triggers. This can be useful, but needs to be carefully controlled as it can have serious performance implications and even lead to looping if the effects propagate back to the original table.

Consequently it is worth reviewing the potential effect of each trigger (propagation analysis).

After all triggers have been defined, derive the trigger hierarchy for each trigger (the worst case of all triggers that could be consequentially affected). Resolve any loops. Assess whether the performance cost is acceptable, and consider ways of limiting any excessive propagation. (Some propagation may be necessary, as in two-level cascade deletes.)

Step 3: Design data notification scheme

If notification strategy 2 (entity level notification) is used, design and build the mechanisms to implement this.

Each entity needs to know about all the components implementing screens or windows (if GUI) that are derived from the entity. Any (relevant) change to the entity is notified to these objects, which update themselves accordingly.

Some databases have special subscription mechanisms to facilitate this. (For example, some DBMSs have a mechanism which enables the designer to define which application components need to be alerted to a particular event.)

If the DBMS supports triggers, an alternative is to build a mechanism for strategy 2 notification using triggers, stored procedures, and additional database tables.

Step 4: Decompose complex procedures

Review the size and complexity of the proposed server procedures. Decompose any large or complex server procedures.

Step 5: Design server update procedures

Server update procedures have already been identified as Event Packages mapped onto the Technical System Architecture.

The procedure may obtain and release write locks as part of the concurrency scheme (the scheme deployed

Chapter 6
Techniques

when many clients attempt to obtain and release the same write locks on data).

If notification strategy 2 is used, it will also send notification messages, either to objects which have registered as part of the notification scheme, or to objects that are simply hard-coded into the procedure. Messages will be sent to components implementing user interface objects containing a view of the data.

If triggers are being used extensively for integrity maintenance, server update procedures will contain little or no code to maintain data integrity. On the other hand, if declarative referential integrity and triggers are not being used, server update procedures are likely to contain much code to maintain referential integrity and to keep redundant and derived data consistent.

Step 6: Design server enquiry procedures

Server enquiry procedures have already been identified as enquiries.

Enquiry procedures are often concerned with producing derived or aggregated data from the stored data, or with merging data from a number of sources.

The procedure may obtain read locks to ensure that the view of the data is consistent or stable.

It may also include subscription requests, to register an interest in an entity so that it is notified of any future updates.

Step 7: Optimise for performance

The Server Design should be optimised as in Step 640 (Optimise Physical Data Design) of core SSADM.

However, there are some specific client/server tuning issues.

Controlled Data Redundancy

Storing redundant data is a standard database tuning technique, but is particularly important in server databases that have stored procedures and triggers.

Database design uses normalisation techniques to eliminate redundancy. However normalisation can increase access times because relational joins have to be

97

performed to recombine related data from different tables. Performance can be improved by storing redundant copies of some data in convenient locations in the DBMS. Use stored procedures and triggers to maintain consistency between the redundant data and the master data.

For example, in a Sales Order processing application, normalisation indicates that the Order table should hold the Customer reference (key), but not the Customer name and address. Every time an Order is printed or displayed on the screen, the name and address are retrieved (using the key) from the Customer table. Performance is improved (at the cost of extra storage) by holding the customer name and address on every Order.

Ensure consistency by having stored procedures that update Order data, but which prevent the user directly changing the redundant name and address. Also use a trigger on the Customer table, such that on update of a Customer name and address, all copies in the Order table are updated in the same way.

A second example is derived data. The total outstanding invoice payments for a Customer can be calculated by retrieving data from the Invoice table. Performance is much improved by maintaining a 'Total Outstanding Invoice Value' column on the Customer. The danger is that this becomes inconsistent with the data it is derived from. This problem is avoided by having triggers on the Invoice table, so that any delete, insert or update to an Invoice causes a consequential amendment to the derived value on the Customer.

6.11 Technical system options

Technical system options for client/server applications proceeds as is usual for core SSADM projects with the following additions:

- the critical technical requirements established during requirements definition provide a set of mandatory requirements against which Technical System Options can be evaluated and selected
- the selected TSO is further defined by the Technical System Architecture which replaces the Technical

Chapter 6
Techniques

Environment Description. The technique of technical architecture definition is explained separately.

SSADM and Client/Server Applications

Annex A: Case study

A1 Introduction

This annex shows how SSADM, extended using the techniques in this manual, can be used for the analysis and design of a client/server system by applying it to the EU–Rent case study.

The structure of this chapter is as follows:

- EU–Rent current system and background
- Requirements Catalogue
- User Catalogue
- Event and Enquiry Packages
- Entity Access Matrix
- Technical System Architecture.

A2 EU–Rent current system

EU–Rent is a fictional car rental company operating in many towns throughout Europe, from 1000 branches of three types:

- major airports (100) – open 16 hours per day, 7 days per week, averaging 1350 rentals per branch per week
- major cities (200) – open 11 hours per day, 6 days per week, averaging 750 rentals per branch per week
- local agencies including hotels and garages (700) – open 11 hours per day, 6 days per week, averaging 165 rentals per branch per week.

EU–Rent has 400 service depots for car maintenance and repairs. Service depots generally serve more than one branch. Cars are kept for one year or 40,000 km, whichever comes first. A car generally has 4 services during its life with EU–Rent.

EU–Rent keeps records of 5,000,000 customers and their rentals including comments about bad experiences with customers. Customers stay on the system until they have been inactive for ten years.

SSADM and Client/Server Applications

A2.1 Current information system

Each branch and/or service depot has a local PC based system including a file server. Most equipment is obsolete and limited in capacity. Hardware failures are increasingly frequent. Application programs have been maintained over several years and amendments are becoming progressively more difficult and expensive.

A copy of the customer blacklist is held at every branch. This is supposed to be updated once a week but due to the logistics of circulating disks this is in practice carried out about every 4 weeks.

A2.2 Co-ordination

Each location operates almost independently of others. Communication is via phone and fax and is very variable. Sometimes when cars are dropped off at different locations, the drop off branch does not inform the pick up branch. Branch managers tend to operate in small groups and not to look for 'spare' cars outside those groups. EU–Rent management feels that some capacity is wasted.

Scheduling of service booking in branch and service depot files is co-ordinated by fax. Sometimes service bookings are not recorded at the branches, and cars booked for services are rented. Sometimes service depots do not know that cars have been transferred to branches served by other depots until another depot requests a service history.

A2.3 Need for new IT system

EU–Rent has decided that a new IT system is required; the existing system cannot be kept going much longer. None of the existing equipment is worth salvaging, although some application code may be re-used if there is a benefit in doing so. Business activity is not expected to change significantly – locations, volumes of rentals and staff are expected to remain stable.

A2.4 EU–Rent operations

Each branch maintains local records of its cars, organized by car group (of which there are 5 levels).

Car rentals

Advance reservations are recorded with a reference, customer details, car group, rental date, and duration. Clerks may reject some reservations based on bad customer experience, such as late returns or car damage.

Annex A
Case study

Customers may cancel reservations at any time until the car is picked up.

Reservations are recorded by car group. Each day, booking clerks look through the rentals due to start on the following day, look for available cars in each group and book a specific car for each reservation.

The branch manager must ensure that there are sufficient cars in each group to meet the reservation demand. The manager may have to contact other branches in order to arrange transfers. In extremes a customer may be given a car from another group.

When a car is picked up the system produces a contract/invoice including a customer copy.

When a car is returned, the time is noted, the customer pays and is given a receipt. Comments may be noted against the customer, and as a result the customer may be blacklisted. Head office maintains a list of blacklisted customers which is distributed to all branches.

A car rented from one branch of EU–Rent may be returned to any other branch. It is the responsibility of the renting branch to ensure that the car has been returned somewhere. If a car is returned to a different branch the 'ownership' of the car is transferred to the new branch. The branch from which the car was rented is notified by telephone or fax.

A customer may walk in and request an immediate rental. If a suitable car is available a booking is made and a contract/invoice is produced as for a reservation.

Car pools

A branch manager may assign a car to the pool by purchasing it using money from head office, or by arranging for one to be transferred from another branch

A branch manager may reduce the car pool by selling a car, or scheduling its transfer to another branch so long as it is not booked for rental or maintenance.

SSADM and Client/Server Applications

A car may be written off at any time, if authorized by the branch manager. If the car is booked for a rental then another car must be booked to replace it.

Only one rental or maintenance booking is allowed per car day. Rental and maintenance bookings may cover several days.

Car transfers
Cars tend to accumulate at some branches (Calais for example). Every so often a branch manager will ring round other branches seeking to gain or lose a few cars. A transfer may be cancelled at any time until the car is picked up. The pick up represents confirmation of the scheduled transfer.

Car movements within EU–Rent
Drivers are hired to pick up the car from the branch for maintenance, or transfer to another branch. The pick up of a car represents confirmation of maintenance or transfer. The time of pick up is noted and the driver is given authorization. When the car is returned, the time is noted and the driver given a receipt.

Maintenance
Each service depot maintains local service records of cars owned by its branches. Maintenance scheduling requires co-ordination between the relevant branch and depot manager, to ensure that records are in step.

Cars are scheduled for servicing every 10,000 km. Service dates are negotiated between relevant managers and are based upon the cars rental schedule (that is a free slot) and the service schedule at the depot.

Administration
Head office administration has a role to play in maintaining basic branch information, for instance archiving dead customers or reinstating customers.

Customers
Customers are identified by driving licence number, so different branches can recognize and deal with the same customers.

Late returns
To check that a car has been returned, the procedure is that every day one of the booking clerks looks through the rentals for rentals due to end the previous day, but for which no return has been noted. The procedure is then to check the compound for the car, to call the

customer and finally to call round all other branches to determine if the car has been returned there instead.

It is clear that the above procedure is tedious and time consuming, which ought to be resolved by providing automatic notification of cars returned to different branches.

A2.5 Information required

Information required at branches consists of:–

- available cars – to see which cars are available to fill reservations and which are available to fill other branch requests
- bookings – to ensure that no double bookings take place
- branch rentals – to identify the cars required for the following days' rentals
- late returns – to contact the customer in order to ascertain why cars have not been returned
- car transfers – to let the branch manager know which cars have been lost from his branch, by being returned to other branches
- maintenance – when a car is transferred, if the car is scheduled to be serviced and the new branch uses a different service depot, to let the branch manager know that he must cancel the service and arrange new bookings.

Information required at service depots consists of:

- car bookings – to see when a car can be serviced
- capacity – to see the available dates for servicing
- history – to have all car history for reference when servicing
- schedule – to have a schedule of all services for the immediate future to support planning.

Information required at the head office consists of:

- car movements – to give an analysis of the movement of cars by transfers and returns to other branches

SSADM and Client/Server Applications

- branch history – to give an analysis of rentals, gains and losses of cars to enable input to decisions such as whether to keep branches open or on staff levels

- car group usage – to give an analysis of rentals and maintenance costs of different car groups

- customers – to enable input on decisions whether to suspend, reinstate or remove customers.

A3 Requirements catalogue

During analysis of EU–Rent's current situation we define the functional and non-functional requirements by investigating the problems which were highlighted when examining the current system.

A3.1 Functional requirements

Tables A1, A2 and A3 contain a selection of EU–Rent functional requirements.

Requirements Catalogue Entry	
Source	Branch Manager
Requirement	To prevent double booking of rental cars from occuring
Benefit	Increased customer satisfaction / reduced staff overload in having to replace cars, easier car management
Comments/Suggested Solutions	On–line access to all bookng information, immediate update when booking takes place
Related Documents	DFM Process 3
Related Requirements	Consistency, Car Transfers
Resolution	

Table A1: Requirements Catalogue entry – number 1

Annex A
Case study

Requirements Catalogue Entry	
Source	Branch Manager
Requirement	To have consistency between rental records at different locations
Benefit	Easier tracking of car location, Faster information on late rental returns at different locations
Comments/Suggested Solutions	On-line access to all rental information, including access to other branch rental information
Related Documents	DFM Process 2, 3 and 4
Related Requirements	Car Transfers, Double booking
Resolution	

Table A2: Requirements Catalogue entry – number 2

Requirements Catalogue Entry	
Source	Head Office
Requirement	To allow an instant check of bad risk customers during bookings and rentals
Benefit	Reduced risk of car mistreatment or loss of revenue due to late returns
Comments/Suggested Solutions	All branches to keep an up to date bad risk customer list which should be referred to during all rentals and reservations. This list should be held centrally and downloaded before commencement of each day's trading
Related Documents	DFM Process 3
Related Requirements	Consistency, Identification of customers
Resolution	

Table A3: Requirements Catalogue entry – number 3

A3.2 Non-functional requirements

Non-functional requirements (NFRs) are extended as shown below as these provide input into the detailed client/server split options.

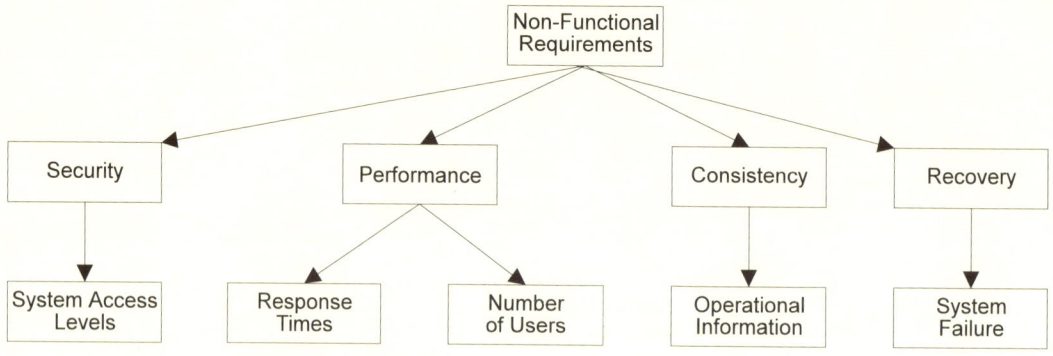

Figure A1: Non-functional requirements structure

The NFR structure diagram (see Figure A1) shows a decomposition of requirement areas into system specific NFRs. Tables A4 and A5 are examples of EU–Rent NFRs.

Non-functional Requirements	
Critical requirement	Yes
Description	To have an acceptable system response time
Quality attribute	Allowable maximum response
Scale	Time (seconds)
Test for achievement	Response time monitoring pre and post implementation
Target level	3 seconds
Tolerances	Up to 5 seconds
Cost of missing target level	Slow system rate for rental/reservations, user frustration
Minimum cost	Not yet calculated

Table A4: Non-functional requirements – number 1

Annex A
Case study

Non-functional Requirements	
Critical requirement	Yes
Description	EU–Rent branch system recovery period (following a software/hardware failure)
Quality attribute	Time to recover system
Scale	Time (minutes)
Test for achievement	To carry out recovery trials before implementation in order to test system recovery times
Target level	15 minutes
Tolerances	5 minutes additional time
Cost of missing target level	Loss of revenue through lack of information/lost reservation
Minimum cost	Calculated at £500 per minute of system down time

Table A5: Non-functional requirements – number 2

A4 User catalogue

In order to ascertain how and where information and processing will be required we must first examine the various types of users that will be in contact with the system, their location, and any specialist workstation requirements that need to be taken into account. These factors will also help when we design the system interface.

A4.1 User definitions

Outlined below are examples of system users at EU–Rent.

Branch manager — The branch managers are responsible for handling day to day branch management issues, co-ordinating staff and controlling the number of cars present at the branch.

Service depot manager — The service depot managers are responsible for controlling the maintenance schedule for all cars falling under the depot's geographic area, managing the service depot and liaising with the local branch managers to arrange car movements.

SSADM and Client/Server Applications

Branch booking clerk
: The branch booking clerks are responsible for dealing with customers, taking reservations, payment and allocating cars.

Customer
: The customers use EU–Rent to rent cars.

: The customer is considered to be an indirect user of the EU–Rent system. Indirect user types should also receive consideration as they may affect the non-functional requirements and style of interface.

A4.2 User classes

The user definitions are so distinct that we can use these as our user classes. Table A6 shows the information required to document user classes.

	Entry 1	Entry 2	Entry 3
Class Name	Branch Manager	Booking Clerk	Customer
Access type	Direct	Direct	Indirect
Frequency	4 / day	40 / day	2 / year
Mand/optional	Mandatory	Mandatory	Mandatory
No of other applications	Lotus 123, PMW	None	None
No of users in type	1000	2500	5,000,000 on record

Table A6: User Class entries

A4.3 Business location types

Having documented the types of users that will interact with the system, consideration must be given to the locations at which the users will operate. These locations are locations from which processing may be triggered, and to which system initiated outputs are delivered.

This will help to give an understanding of the processing requirements at each location. These requirements will be broken down further during event/enquiry analysis.

There are three different business location types at EU–Rent. These are outlined in Table A7.

	Entry 1	Entry 2	Entry 3
ID	LOC001	LOC002	LOC003
Name	Head Office	Branch Office	Service Depot
No of locations	1	1000	400
Description	The central office for senior management and strategic control of the business	Handles all business operations including car rental related tasks, plus car tranfers and purchases	Carries out all car maintenance and scheduling for services
Function XREF	Manage Customers, Manage Car Groups, Manage Branches, Manage Service Depots, Analyse Car Movements	Book Car, Sell Car, Transfer Car, Rental Return, Customer Pickup, Purchase Car, Check Late Returns, Walk in Rental	Maintenance Schedule, Remove Old Entries, Take Maintenance Booking, Cancel Maintenance Booking
User XREF	System Support, H.O. Management	Branch Clerk Branch Manager Customers	Service Depot Manager

Table A7: Business Location Type entries

A4.4 Workstation types

In examination of the various workstation types required at EU–Rent taking into account any specialist needs, three types are identified:

- sales workstations
- service depots
- head office workstations.

See Table A8 for the information to be documented when considering the type of hardware required for the system. Note that Workstation Types are all cross-referenced to business locations.

	Type 1	Type 2	Type 3
Name	Sales Workstation	Service Depot	Head Office Workstation
ID	WS001	WS002	WS003
Description	Used as the medium to create all rentals/take all reservations from customers	Used to arrange maintenance schedules for cars	Used to provide head office with management information and for support to maintain the information held upon the system
Specialist Use	Should be a GUI with high resolution graphics in order to enhance customer perception of the company	Should be durable due to the working environment of the workstation (ie busy workshop)	Should have a large screen to accomodate accounts information
Business Location	LOC002	LOC003	LOC001

Figure A8: Workstation Types

Specialist workstation requirements feed into the client platform solution. The chosen platform should be capable of accommodating any specialist requirements that have been justified.

A5 Event and Enquiry Packages

Using the events for EU–Rent (which would have been previously defined during function definition) we can now look at each event in turn and determine the Business Location Type at which the event/enquiry takes place.

These events and enquiries will then be used during system specification and physical design.

Annex A
Case study

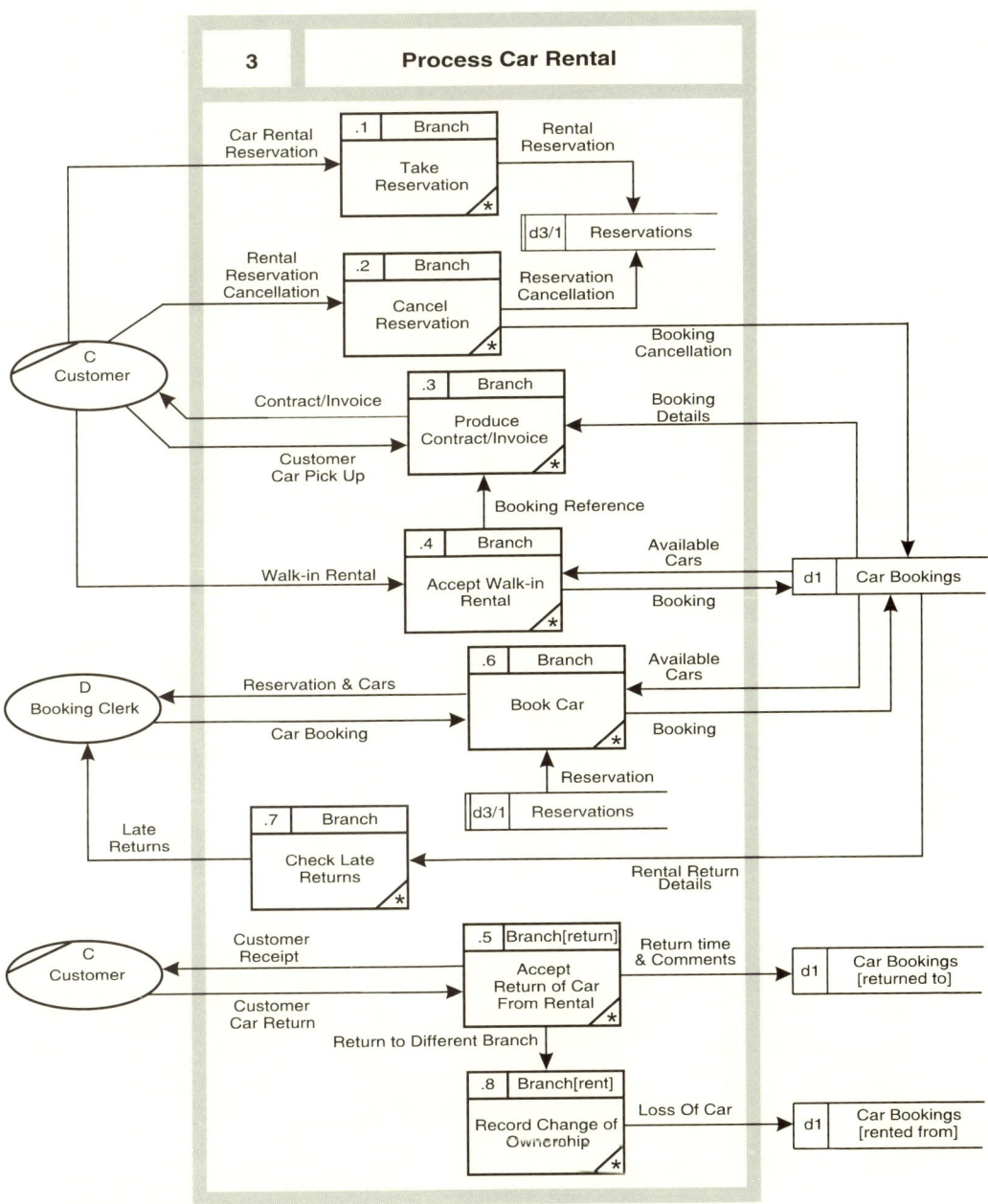

Figure A2: DFD 'Rental'

SSADM and Client/Server Applications

A5.1 Snapshot from function definition stage

From Figure A2 we can define the functions required for EU–Rent for the rental processing that the system will handle.

These functions are then mapped into the events and enquiries derived from the Entity Access Matrix (see Table A9).

Function	Event /Enquiry
Book Car	Available cars Renatal booking
Cancel reservation	Rental cancellation
Check late returns	Late returns for branch
Customer pick up	Rental pick–up
Renturn from rental	Rental return Scheduled maintenance
Take reservation	Reservation
Walk in rental	Available cars Walk in rental

Table A9: Extract from Function to Event/Enquiry mapping

A5.2 Event/Enquiry detail

Tables A10 to A12 show a selection of events from the EU–Rent 'rental' processing area.

Event	Walk in rental
Associated function(s)	Walk in rental
Description	To create a rental for a customer who does not have a reservation
Mode	Critical Online
Frequency	3300 per day
Business Location	Frequency
Major Branch Office	1300 per day
Branch Office	2000 per day

Table A10: Event detail number 1

Event	Reservation
Associated function(s)	Take reservation
Description	To take a reservation from a customer for a future car rental
Mode	Critical Online
Frequency	65000 per day
Business Location	Frequency
Major Branch Office	35000 per day
Branch Office	30000 per day

Table A11: Event detail number 2

Event	Rental booking
Associated function(s)	Book car Write off car
Description	To allocate a car in order to satisfy either a reservation or a walk in rental
Mode	Online
Frequency	70000 per day
Business Location	Frequency
Major Branch Office	50000 per day
Branch Office	20000 per day

Table A12: Event detail number 3

Table A13 is an example of an enquiry from 'rental' processing area.

Enquiry	Available cars
Associated function(s)	Record agreement for transfer Book car Write off car Walk in rental
Description	To check the local car data-base to locate the available cars for a particular group
Mode	Online
Frequency	10000 per day
Business Location	Frequency
Major Branch Office	5000 per day
Branch Office	5000 per day

Table A13: Enquiry detail number 4

A6   Entity Access Matrix

Taking each entity from the EU–Rent Logical Data Model (see Figure A3), we can now document the effects of any events and enquiries upon these entities by composing an Entity Access Matrix.

The Entity Access Matrix will then help us to ascertain the information that each event requires and by doing so will help us to decide at which location the data and processing should sit upon the system.

The Entity Access Matrix shown in Table A14 demonstrates how the events and enquiries for 'rental' are combined into one matrix.

Annex A
Case study

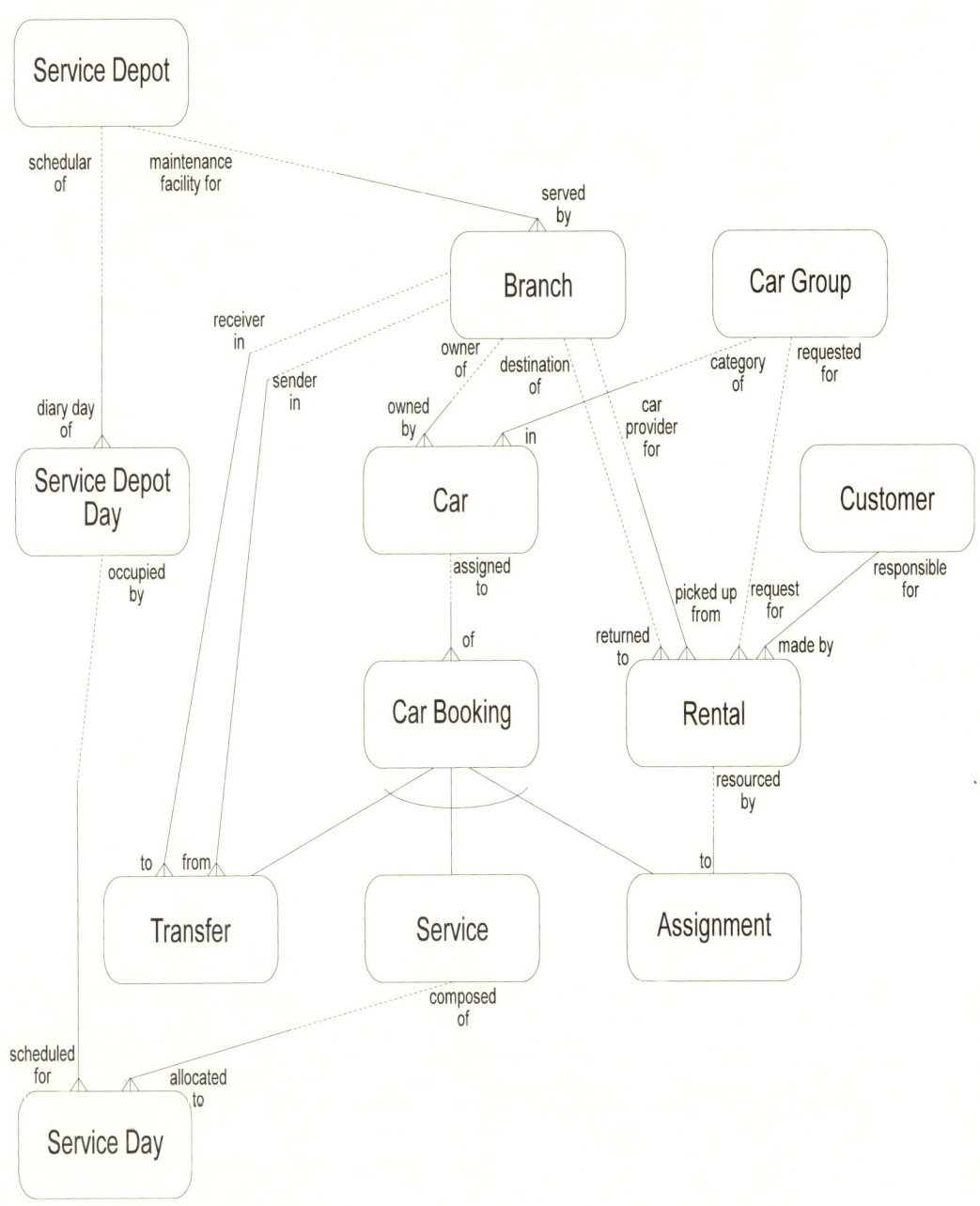

Figure A3: EU-Rent Logical Data Model

SSADM and Client/Server Applications

Event / Enquiry	Assign-ment	Branch	Car	Car Group	Customer	Rental	Service	Service Depot	Transfer
Available Cars	R	R	R	R			R		R
Late Returns	R	R	R		R	R			
Rental Booking	C		R	R		C			
Rental Cancellation	D		R	R	M	D			
Rental Return	D	R	R			D			
Reservation		R		R	M,C	C			
Scheduled Maint		R	R				R	R	
Walk-in Rental	C	R	R	R	C,M	C			

Table A14: Entity Access Matrix (scoped to 'Rental')

A7 Distribution Option

EU–Rent decided on almost separate systems for rentals and maintenance.

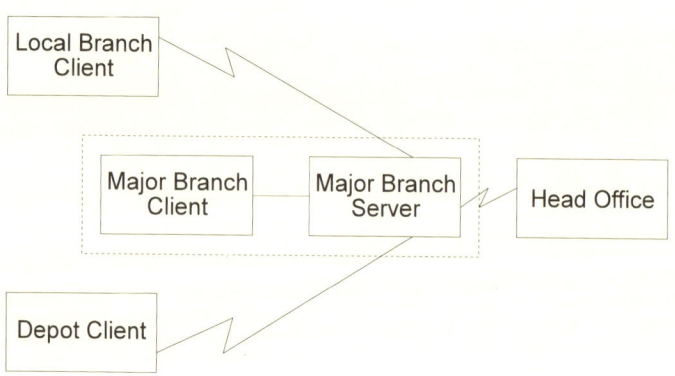

Figure A4: High level client/server map for EU–Rent branches

In the rentals system there will be client workstations at each branch and servers at each major branch (city and airport). Each city branch will support a small number of local agency branches. Branch servers will hold car and rental data: customer data will be held on a central server at head office (see Figure A4).

Service depots will be able to access branch servers to book cars for service.

Annex A
Case study

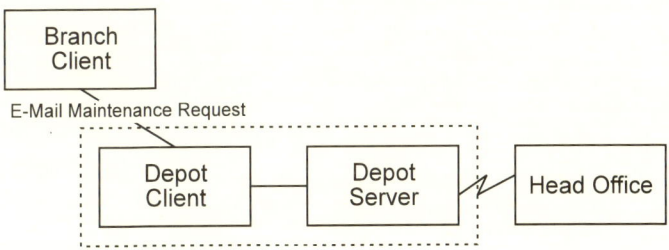

Figure A5: EU–Rent maintenance client/server map showing major data flows for car maintenance

Although each branch server will be co-ordinated with head office, branch servers will remain unco-ordinated with respect to each other.

In the maintenance system (see Figure A5) each depot will have its own server, which will maintain the work schedule for the depot and the service histories of its 'local' cars. The head office server will hold details of the branches served by each depot.

Generally, depots will not need to be co-ordinated, except when cars change ownership.

There will be no automatic co-ordination between depot and branch servers. A depot client may receive E–mail messages from branch clients (such as requesting cars for service), but the user at the depot will be responsible for reacting to them. A depot client will make service bookings on both branch and depot servers, but they will be on separate commit units, if one fails, the client will cancel the other.

A8	**Technical System Architecture**	The following documentation describes the components of both the hardware and software infrastructure necessary to support the client/server solution for EU–Rent.
A8.1	**Platform Description**	Table A15 is an example of EU–Rent's chosen hardware and software platform for the client platform.

SSADM and Client/Server Applications

ID: PLAT001	Layer: DATA	~~client~~/**server**
Description: SYBASE RDBMS running upon ICL DRS 6000 mini-computer.			

Component: SYBASE RDBMS
Cornerstone component?: Yes
Reason for selection: High performance rating for comparative cost/ability to meet Rqmt Spec.
 	
Availability: 5am – 10pm
Procurement cost:
Skills required: DBA
Training costs: £10,000
Standards:
Dependency upon other components:
  UNIX
  ICL DRS computer
Application software:
  To be defined
Workstation types:			

Table A15: Platform Description

A8.2 Message Channel Description

Table A16 is an example of the chosen message channel handling protocol in order to meet specification from the Requirements Catalogue. One of the key considerations was EU–Rent's non-functional requirement for a fast response time.

Name: TCP/IP comms protocol
Description: Standard TCP connection via PSDN
Connecting platforms: ICL DRS – PC **Transmission rates:** Min: 9600bpm Max: 19200bpm Mean: 14400bpm
Response times: 2 seconds average
Transmission cost: 5p per unit
Error correction provision: Even parity check
Outside agency dependency: PSDN

Table A16: Message Channel Description

Annex A
Case study

A8.3 Standard mapping

Figure A6 shows the standard mapping describing the general client/server split for EU–Rent. This first cut is based upon high level information and processing requirements at each location. This provides a 'cornerstone' from which to base our entire system mapping. There may be exceptions to this mapping; these will be documented when we detail each client/server design instance. (See section A9).

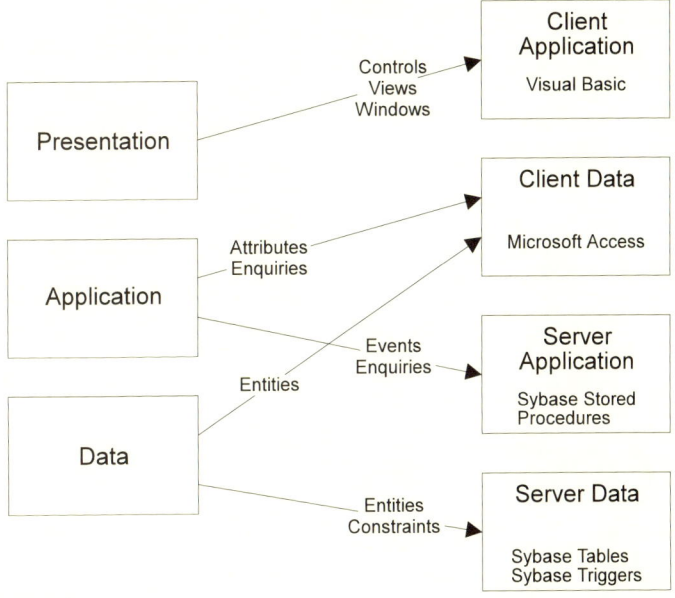

Figure A6: EU–Rent standard mapping

A9 Client/server design

We can now begin to fully detail precisely where our design objects will sit on our system. Taking each design object in turn, we must now consider if the standard mapping satisfies all the non-functional requirements (see Tables A17 to A20). Where these requirements are not met we should document any mapping exceptions that must exist.

One of the major non-functional requirements for EU–Rent is robustness – if a local agency has a car in the car park and a customer who wants it, the agency wants to be able to raise a contract, even if the server at the city branch is out of communication. This first design instance shows how we would accommodate this requirement.

Specification instance: customer (entity)	
Platform component: Sybase table	
Mapping exceptions:	
Non-functional requirement	Mapping explanation
NFR01 – response times	Customer entity also held at local branch within MS Access (downloaded from the server each morning)
NFR04 – robustness	As above

Table A17: Client/server design – Customer (entity)

Specification instance: rental (event)	
Platform component: Sybase stored procedure	
Mapping exceptions:	
Non-functional requirement	Mapping explanation
NFR02 – system recovery	Operational critical events/enquiries to be held within Visual Basic to allow processing whilst network connection is off–line.

Table A18: Client/server design – Rental (event)

Annex A
Case study

Specification instance: branch (entity)	
Platform component: Sybase table	
Mapping exceptions:	
Non-functional requirement	Mapping explanation
None	None

Table A19: Client/server design – Branch (entity)

Table A20 documents the special components that will be required.

Special component: notification strategy	
Platform component: notification trigger	
Mapping exceptions:	
Non-functional requirement	Mapping explanation
NFR03 – consistency	Optimistic locking. Update on–line all rental objects when changes are made. Broadcast message to users using those objects allowing changes to be saved.

Table A20: Client/server design – special components

SSADM and Client/Server Applications

Bibliography

Information Systems The Information Systems Engineering Library is available
Engineering Library from HMSO Publications Centre, PO Box 276, London
SW8 5DT

The following volumes are referenced in this publication or are particularly relevant:

- SSADM and GUI Design: A Project Manager's Guide
  ISBN: 0 95 221530 6

- Distributed Systems: Application Development
  ISBN: 0 11 330623 7

- Customising SSADM
  ISBN: 0 11 330664 4

SSADM Documentation The SSADM Version 4 Reference Manual is published by NCC Blackwell Ltd and is available from NCC Blackwell Ltd, 108 Cowley Road, Oxford OX4 1JF.

ISBN: 1 85554 004 5

SSADM and Client/Server Applications

Glossary

3–schema specification architecture (3–SSA)	A framework or IT system specification and implementation, in which the IS services needed to support business activities are defined in a Conceptual Model. The mappings from the Conceptual Model to specific user organisations and implementation technologies are defined in an External Design and an Internal Design.
Architecture	The structure of the system software components that provide basic services to applications. The usage of 'Architecture' is distinct as from the usage in the 3–schema specification architecture.
business area modelling	The process of identifying Business Location Types and Workstation Type
Business Location Type	A geographically distinct site where particular subsets of business activity are to which user populations are assigned.
client/server partitioning	Describes how to transform a client/server application logical design into a physical design for a specific client/server architecture.
client design	The detailed design and development of the client software components.
Commit	Part of transaction processing when a series of data updates grouped together in a single transaction are confirmed to the database.
Conceptual Model	The Conceptual Schema in the 3–schema specification srchitecture is called a *Model* to emphasise that it is a partial model of the business, developed by a process of analysis and discovery. It specifies such required IT services as: information support needed by business activities; data needed to provide it; processes needed to keep the data up to date. It also defines which business activities are to be automated. It describes the services independently of the user organisation structure and the technology for implementation.

critical technical requirement	A subset of non-functional requirements that place major constraints or demands on the technical infrastructure of the system.
Distribution Option	A presentation of an approach to the distribution of system functionality (expressed as events and enquiries) across the available system platforms.
DLL	Dynamic Linked Library.
Entity Access Matrix	A table showing how events and enquiries affect Logical Data Model entities. It shows which entities are inserted to, deleted from, modified and read.
Entity-event modelling	The name given to the collective creation of Event and Enquiry Packages. The procedure related to Entity Life Histories remains as defined in core SSADM.
Enquiry Package	Details about an enquiry with its Enquiry Access Map (EAP) showing how data is retrieved from a Data Model.
Event Package	Details about an event with its Effect Correspondence Diagram (ECD) showing how data is manipulated on a Data Model.
External Design	The External Design in the 3–schema specification architecture, called a *Design* to emphasise that it is developed by a process of design and engineering. The External Schema passes update data and enquiry triggers to the Conceptual Model, and receives update and query output as a response.
Internal Design	The Internal Design in the 3–schema specification architecture, called a *Design* to emphasise that it is developed by a process of design and engineering. The Logical Data Model in the Conceptual Model is mapped on to a data storage and access technology to produce a database design. Stored data is presented to implement update and Enquiry process by a processes data interface, as if it were stored in the Logical Data Model.

Glossary

GUI	Graphical User Interface – a human computer interface adhering to the WIMP (windows, icons, menus and pointers) paradigm.
Message Channel	A connection between two Platforms that is capable of transferring messages, eg a Local Area Network, a modem connection, or a Datex_P connection.
Non-functional requirements	Requirements based on factors such as performance, data integrity and data quality.
Platform Description	Identifies any available hardware/software platform and defines the services that it will offer the logical/conceptual system.
RDBMS	Relational Database Management System.
remote procedure call	A request from a client to a server usually over a network.
Rollback	Part of transaction processing when a series of data updates grouped together in a single transaction are not committed and the data is returned to its state before the beginning of the transaction.
server design	The detailed design and development of the server software components.
Standard Mapping	Defines on which platform each element of the system's conceptual schema (ie LDM, events, enquiries) and user interface will be supported.
Task Model	Definition of multiple, textual, job activity descriptions or references to a set of User Tasks.
Technical System Architecture	A description of the components of the hardware and software infrastructure necessary to support the client/server application.
Transaction	A unit of business or Conceptual Model processing that must succeed or fail as a unit.
Trigger	An event that triggers common processing within the server data management system (eg an RDBMS).

Stored Procedure   A common procedure or piece of processing incumbent in the Server data management system (eg an RDBMS), that can be called remotely from the client.

User Catalogue   An extension to the User Catalogue defined in SSADM, it also includes information about User Classes and the geographical sites at which the job is performed.

Workstation Type   The capabilities of a kind of workstation.

Index

3GL 26
3–schema specification architecture (3–SSA) 24, 25, 42, 43, 72, 127
4GL 21, 22, 26, 38

application logic 16, 17
application function logic 15
Application Programming Interface 61

business area modelling 36, 71, 75-77, 85, 127
business logic 18, 21, 78, 95
Business Location Types 23, 35, 36, 37, 41, 48, 49, 50-55, 57, 61, 69, 74, 80, 84, 77, 79, 84, 88, 89, 110, 111, 112, 127
Business System Options 23, 35, 47, 49, 64, 65

CASE 10, 22, 44, 52,80, 84, 88, 96, 101
client application layer 26, 28
client design 15, 22, 26, 39, 40, 71, 75, 77, 79, 90-92, 127
client presentation layer 26
client process 14, 20
client/server partitioning 15-18, 22, 26, 40, 71, 75, 79, 83, 85, 89-93, 127
Client/Server Design 23, 29, 39, 40, 41, 42, 50, 66-68, 74, 75, 86, 89, 91, 93, 121-123
commit 18, 19, 119, 127
Conceptual Model 24, 25, 60, 67, 127-129
Context Diagram 51, 53, 54
cornerstone component 63, 88, 89, 120
critical technical requirement 45, 91, 128
Current Physical Data Flow Model 51, 53, 54

data integrity 22, 34, 43, 94, 97, 129
data access logic 15, 21
database 10, 13, 14, 16-18, 21, 28, 33, 34, 58, 64, 86, 91, 94-97, 127-129
DBMS 16, 22, 39, 42, 93, 94, 96, 98
DBMS Performance Classification 42
DBMS Storage Classification 42
developers 30
dialogue design 38
distribute 15
distributed application 16, 17, 81
distributed data access 16
distributed processing 14, 23
distribution 37, 38, 41, 47-49, 61, 74, 90, 118, 128
Distribution Option 38, 41, 47-49, 61, 118, 128
downsize 21
Dynamic Linked Libraries (DDL) 26, 67

Effect Correspondence Diagram (ECD) 36, 38, 42, 55, 56, 58, 84, 128
enquiry 28, 36, 38, 41, 57-60, 67, 68, 73, 78, 80, 83-86, 90-93, 95, 97, 101, 110, 112, 114, 116, 118, 128
Enquiry Package 36
Enquiry Access Paths (EAP) 36, 41, 57, 58, 78, 84, 128
Enquiry Package 41, 57, 58, 67, 68,128
Entity Life Histories (ELH) 36, 56, 58, 78, 80, 128
entity-event modelling 36, 55, 71, 77, 78, 80, 85, 90, 128
event 23, 28, 36, 38, 41, 42, 48, 55, 56, 58, 59, 67, 68, 71, 74, 77-86, 90-96, 101, 110, 112, 114-116, 118, 122,128, 129
Event Access Matrix 41
Event Package 42, 55, 56, 67, 68, 128
Event/Entity Matrix 36, 41, 58, 59, 78
External Design 24, 25, 60, 62, 127, 128

feasibility study 33, 34
Feasibility Module 33
function 15, 34, 36, 39, 40, 42, 49, 51, 52, 55-59, 79, 80, 83, 111, 112, 114-116
function definition 55-58, 79, 80, 83, 112, 114
Function Component Implementation Map (FCIM) 39, 40, 42

I/O Structures 36
integrity constraints 38, 39, 93, 95
Internal Design 9, 24, 25, 52, 67, 127, 128

layering 14, 25
legacy systems 16, 21
Logical Data Model (LDM) 23, 35, 39, 48, 49, 51, 53, 54, 56, 58, 59, 66-68, 78-80, 116, 117, 128, 129
Logical System Specification 55, 57

Message Channel Description 61, 65, 120
messages 14, 16, 65, 92, 97, 119, 129

network 14, 17-19, 65, 88, 122, 129
node 19, 45, 56, 76
non-functional requirements (NFRs) 23, 29, 30, 31, 33-35, 42-44, 47, 50, 60, 67, 69, 72, 74, 75, 76, 83, 87, 89, 91, 106, 108-110, 121, 128
notification scheme 38, 39, 68, 96, 97

PC 13, 14, 15, 21, 26, 28, 102, 120
Physical Design 22, 25-27, 26, 28, 39, 40, 41, 55, 57, 90, 112, 127
Physical Environment Classification 42
physical process specification 71, 90, 93
pilot project 22
platform 16, 18, 29, 37, 39, 41, 42, 48, 61-64, 66-68, 79, 83, 86-88, 112, 119, 120, 122, 123
Platform Description 37, 41, 42, 61, 62, 64, 67, 119, 120, 129
presentation logic 15, 21
presentation layer 16, 26
PRINCE 29
processing roles 14, 16, 18
Processing Specification 36, 49, 58, 59
Processing System Classification 42
project scope 34
project manager 9, 10, 29-31, 77, 125
Project Initiation Document (PID) 33, 51, 53, 54
prototyping 21 30, 38, 61, 85

133

RDBMS 21, 28, 63, 120, 129, 130
referential integrity rules 28
relational database management system 28, 129
remote procedure calls 14, 20, 22, 27, 93
remote transaction management 18
requirements definition 34, 35, 71, 72, 74, 76, 77, 85, 98
Requirements Catalogue 23, 34, 35, 42-44, 46, 47, 49, 51, 53, 54, 56, 58, 59, 61, 64, 65, 74, 83, 101, 106, 107, 120
Requirements Specification 23, 34, 35, 37, 50, 78
roles 14, 16, 18, 23, 51, 53
rollback 129

schemas 24
server application layer 28
server data layer 28
server design 15, 22, 23, 26, 27, 29, 39, 40, 41, 42, 50, 66-68, 71, 74, 75, 79, 86, 89, 91-93, 95, 97, 121-123, 129
server process 13, 14, 20
SSADM 9-12, 22-24, 26, 29, 33-35, 37, 38, 41, 42, 44, 46, 47, 49, 50, 52, 53, 55-58, 60, 62, 65-67, 69, 71, 72, 74-80, 84-86, 90, 92, 97, 98,101, 125, 128, 130
Stage 0 33
Stage 1 34
Stage 2 35
Stage 3 34, 35
Stage 4 33, 37, 38, 40
Stage 5 38
Stage 6 36, 39
Standard Mapping 22, 37, 39, 41, 61, 62, 66-68, 79, 85, 89-91, 93, 121, 129
Step 010 33
Step 020 34
Step 030 34
Step 040 34
Step 110 34
Step 120 34
Step 130 35
Step 140 35
Step 150 35
Step 160 35
Step 210 35
Step 220 35
Step 310 35
Step 320 36

Step 330 36
Step 340 36
Step 350 36
Step 360 36
Step 370 37
Step 380 37
Step 410 37, 39
Step 420 38
Step 430 38
Step 440 38
Step 510 38
Step 520 38
Step 530 38
Step 540 39
Step 610 39
Step 620 39
Step 630 39, 40
Step 640 40, 92, 97
Step 650 40
Step 660 40
Step 670 40
stored procedures 22, 28, 93, 95-98
structural model 11, 12, 33
structure diagrams 44, 47
System Deveopment Template (SDT) 23, 25, 42, 43, 71, 72

Task Model 41, 46, 50, 51, 53, 54, 69, 129
technical architecture definition 17, 37, 38, 40, 68, 71, 75, 77, 79, 84, 85, 90, 99
Technical Environment Description 37, 42, 85, 86, 98, 101, 119
Technical System Architecture 37, 41-44, 47, 49, 60-62, 65-68, 79, 85-90, 92, 96, 98, 129
technical system options 33, 37, 38, 71, 76, 85, 98
TP 22, 93
transaction 17-19, 22, 46, 92, 127, 129
transaction processing 18, 22, 127, 129
triggers 22, 27, 28, 38, 39, 93-98, 128, 129
TSO 85, 98
two-phase commit 19

User Catalogue 42, 46, 49-52, 61, 64, 65, 69, 101, 109, 130
user classes 50-54, 77, 130
User Environment Model 53
user interface 10, 14, 20, 21, 25, 26, 48, 66-68, 86, 87, 90-92, 97, 101, 129
user roles 23, 51, 53
users 9, 20, 21, 23, 24, 30, 33, 34, 36, 47, 50-54, 56, 58, 69, 73, 74, 77, 109, 110, 123

Workstation Type 41, 51, 53, 54, 127, 130